SAINT PATRICK'S DREAMS INTERPRETED

SAINT PATRICK'S DREAMS INTERPRETED

SEVEN FROM GOD - ONE FROM SATAN - THREE
ABOUT SPEAKING IN TONGUES

❦

BRENDAN MC CAULEY

Copyright © 2024 by Brendan Mc Cauley

All rights reserved.

No part of this book may be reproduced in any form or by any electronic or mechanical means, including information storage and retrieval systems, without written permission from the author, except for the use of brief quotations in a book review.

For Laurence & Rosanne McDowell

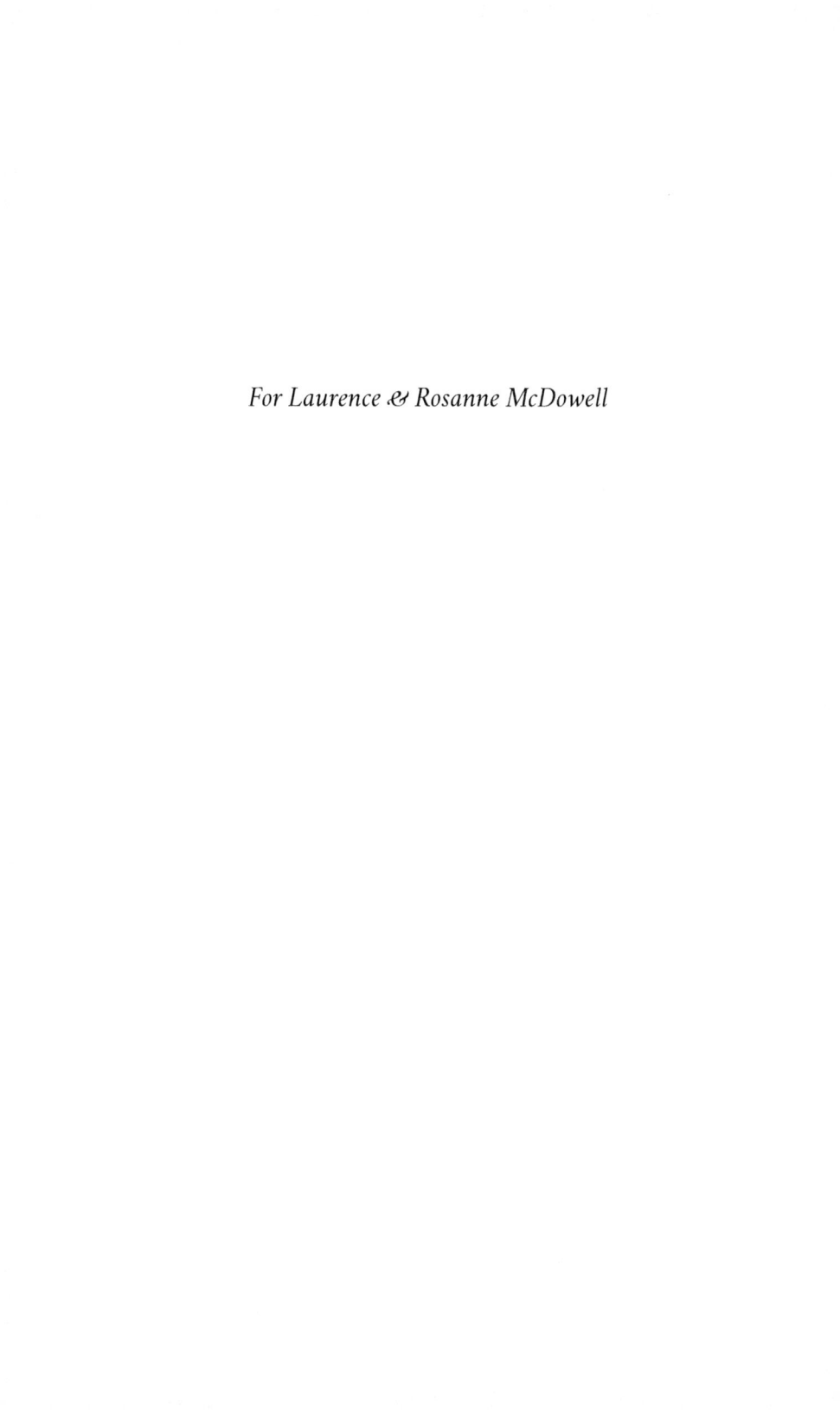

We are the music makers,
    And we are the dreamers of dreams,
Wandering by lone sea-breakers,
    And sitting by desolate streams; —
World-losers and world-forsakers,
    On whom the pale moon gleams:
Yet we are the movers and shakers
    Of the world for ever, it seems.

Arthur O'Shaughnessy

In the last days, says the Lord, I will pour out my Spirit on all flesh, and your sons and your daughters will prophesy; your young people will see visions and your older people will dream dreams.

Saint Patrick (quoting Joel 2 and Acts 2)

CONTENTS

1. The Burj al Arab In Green — 1
2. Saints & Scholars — 3
3. The World's Favourite Saint — 9
4. Two Saint Patricks — 13
5. The Holy Spirit — 17
6. Patrick's Simple Story — 21
7. St Patrick's Eight Dreams — 23
8. How Jesus Interprets Dreams — 27
9. Notes On Patrick's Dreams — 41
10. Praying In Tongues Dreams — 53
11. Six Sources Of Dreams — 61
12. Dream Interpreter Patrick — 77
13. Under The Microscope — 79
14. St Patrick's Metron — 83
15. The McCauley Dream Checklist — 87
16. St Patrick's First Dream 'You Have Fasted Well' — 97
17. St Patrick's Second Dream 'Your Ship Is Ready' — 105
18. St Patrick's Third Dream 'Satan Tested Patrick' — 113
19. St Patrick's Fourth Dream 'Two Months In Captivity' — 129
20. St Patrick's Fifth Dream 'The Call of The Irish' — 135
21. St Patrick's Sixth Dream 'Jesus Speaks Within You' — 141
22. St Patrick's Seventh Dream 'The Spirit Helps Our Weakness' — 151
23. St Patrick's Eighth Dream 'God's Displeasure' — 165

24. Another Dream?   173
25. The Dreams Scriptures   177

   Notes   187

THE BURJ AL ARAB IN GREEN

SIXTEEN CENTURIES ago God used a young careless Roman citizen to bring the gospel of Jesus Christ to a nation steeped in druidism, slavery, and human sacrifice. A pagan people who worshipped over three hundred gods and goddesses.

Have you ever wondered why each year the whole world celebrates this unlikely man's life? Even a major Muslim city-state like Dubai honours his memory by greening the Burj al Arab, one of the world's most luxurious hotel complexes and the Burj Khalifa, the world's tallest tower on his feast day.

Is it because of the man? Is it because of the nation?

Or is there something else? Is God trying to tell us something? Might this man and this nation still play a part in God's sovereign end time plans and purpose for humanity?

SAINTS & SCHOLARS

ALL HISTORY IS a record of Sovereign Almighty God fulfilling His eternal plans and purpose and the created angel Satan failing to stop Him. The key word is purpose, not purposes, and the purpose is Jesus Christ.

In order to help His people accomplish His plans and purpose God has given us various gifts and callings. Paul told Timothy,

> Every good gift and every perfect gift is from above, coming down from the Father of lights, with whom there is no variation or shadow due to change.[1]

Romans says, For God's gifts and His call can never be withdrawn[2]. This means God won't change His mind about what He has called any one of us to do. If God has called us then that calling is still there, whether or not we have obeyed. And if God has assigned us gifts then those gifts are still available to enable us to accomplish God's plans and purpose for our lives.

Paul encouraged Timothy to stir up the gift within him. He said, For this reason I remind you to fan into flame the gift of God, which is in you through the laying on of my hands.[3]

God is a generous God of abundance and variety. He is more than willing and able to equip us for every good work. You've probably heard about the gifts of the Holy Spirit but there are gifts from each member of the Godhead. They are,

- The Gifts of God,
- The Gifts of Christ
- The Gifts of the Holy Spirit.

The greatest gift of God is eternal life in Christ Jesus our Lord.[4] Isaiah mentions other gifts like the Spirit of wisdom and of understanding, the Spirit of counsel and of might, the Spirit of the knowledge and fear of the Lord.[5]

Scripture says children are a gift from God.[6] A good wife is a gift from God.[7] Food and a good appetite are gifts from God.[8] Good friends are a gift from God.[9] Every good thing that leads to life is a gift from God.[10]

Paul mentions the *Gifts of Christ* in Ephesians,

So Christ himself gave the apostles, the

> prophets, the evangelists, the pastors and teachers, to equip his people for works of service, so that the body of Christ may be built up until we all reach unity in the faith and in the knowledge of the Son of God and become mature, attaining to the whole measure of the fullness of Christ.[11]

These five unique gifts from Jesus are people He has chosen to function in a leadership role within His local and global church. Their main purpose is to equip the saints for the work of ministry as they mature in Christ.

And then, there are the *Gifts of the Holy Spirit*. Paul mentions nine of them in 1 Corinthians.

> There are different kinds of gifts, but the same Spirit distributes them. There are different kinds of service, but the same Lord. There are different kinds of working, but in all of them and in everyone it is the same God at work. Now to each one the manifestation of the Spirit is given for the common good.
> To one there is given through the Spirit a message of wisdom, to another a message of knowledge by means of the same Spirit, to another faith by the

> same Spirit, to another gifts of healing by that one Spirit, to another miraculous powers, to another prophecy, to another distinguishing between spirits, to another speaking in different kinds of tongues, and to still another the interpretation of tongues.
>
> All these are the work of one and the same Spirit, and he distributes them to each one, just as he determines.[12]

There are other Holy Spirit gifts. In Corinthians, Paul mentions helps and administrations.[13] In Romans, He speaks of serving, teaching, exhortation, giving, leadership and mercy.[14] Peter highlights the gifts of speaking and the gifts of serving.[15]

Joel 2:28 and Acts 2:1-4 speak of the gifts of dreams and visions which brings us back to St Patrick.

Although this study focuses on the eight dreams of St Patrick it's important from the outset to realise Patrick was not the only game in town. He was only a very small part of what God was doing on the earth.

God is not in the business of one man ministries. We are all part of the body of Christ. We all have a role to play. There are always seven thousand others who haven't bowed the knee to Baal.[16]

St Patrick wasn't the first person to bring Christianity to Ireland. Christian sailors and traders regularly visited from other nations and there were hundreds, perhaps thousands, of other Christian slaves like Patrick.

There were also well known saints before Patrick, such as Ailbhe, Ciarán, Iban and Declan. In 431 a year before Patrick arrived, Pope St. Celestine I sent Bishop Palladius to shepherd and organise the dispersed Irish Christians but we know little more about him.

Although Patrick wasn't Ireland's first missionary his ministry was effective and memorable. Historians estimate his work resulted in thousands of converts being baptised, over three hundred bishops ordained, and hundreds of churches erected.

Ireland is a breeding ground for saints. There are over four hundred named Irish saints, and that's only those the Pope recognised. Ireland was and still is a fertile land for ascetics, hermits, pioneers, mystics, healers, and all manner of believers.

It's still a land of saints and scholars full of holy people and holy books.

THE WORLD'S FAVOURITE SAINT

St Patrick never drank green beer nor ate corned beef and cabbage. He never supped Guinness and he never drove all the snakes out of Ireland that immediately swam off to America and became politicians and policemen. That's fake news.

Instead, he did something more important. St Patrick left two pieces of authentic Christian writing similar to the epistles of St Paul.

These are called the *Confessio* and the *Epistola (or Letter) to Coroticus*, both in Latin. They can be read in English for free at https://www.confessio.ie

Please read them. It won't take you more than half an hour.

The only reason we know anything about St Patrick

is because a couple of satanic attacks resulted in him writing two articles. Some senior British clergymen discovered Patrick had sinned as a youth and tried to use this information to hinder and discredit his Irish ministry. Their accusations resulted in Patrick scratching his defence on a piece of calf skin that became known as *The Confession*.

Another time, British Christian slave traders killed some of the husbands and sons of Patrick's newly baptised converts and sold the grieving women into slavery. Patrick again put his thoughts on vellum and this became known as *The Letter to the Soldiers of Coroticus*.

From this letter we learn Patrick was a fearless campaigner against slavery and sex trafficking in the fifth century. He willingly risked his life in being a strong Christian voice against slavery. This was 1,500 years before the English evangelical Christian, William Wilberforce, received the same revelation and was bold enough to speak it out.

The British Empire only abolished slavery in 1807, and many of their slaves weren't freed until thirty years later. The United States of America waited another thirty before they saw the light.

Slavery and sex trafficking weren't just theological issues for Patrick. He personally was a victim of slavery. Patrick had strong opinions on human trafficking. He said those murderous slavers were blood stained fellow-citizens of demons, because of their evil works.

He also said they'd face the eternal pains of Hell alongside the devil. He told them, You hand over the members of Christ as it were to a brothel and you divide out defenceless baptised women as prizes.[1]

TWO SAINT PATRICKS

There are two Saint Patricks. There is the real Patrick, the humble missionary, from the fifth century, who left two credible pieces of writing and the Patrick of legend who was fabricated by the seventh century Irish hagiographic spin-doctors, Muirchú and Tírechán and later reinvented by every Tom, Dick and Harry with an agenda.

Modern historians agree this hagiographical revisionism was an attempt to establish Armagh as the ecclesiastical capital of Ireland, and Patrick as its primate.

Wikipedia says,

> A hagiography is an idealised biography of a preacher, priest, founder, saint, monk, nun or icon in any of the

world's religions. Christian hagiographies focus on the lives, and notably the miracles, ascribed to men and women canonised by the Roman Catholic church, the Eastern Orthodox Church, the Oriental Orthodox churches, and the Church of the East.

Hagiographic works, especially those of the Middle Ages, can incorporate a record of institutional and local history, and evidence of popular cults, customs, and traditions.

However, when referring to modern, non-ecclesiastical works, the term hagiography is often used today as a pejorative reference to biographies and histories whose authors are perceived to be uncritical or excessively reverential toward their subject.[1]

It's easy to see the development from history to hagiography in the story of St Patrick. The simple Christian man who described himself an ignorant yokel suddenly became Holy Patrick in the hagiographies.

Also, the miracles of *The Confession* expand greatly in the hagiographies. In *The Confession* the miracles point to God while the hagiographers use them to glorify Patrick. Patrick's personal writing emphasised persecution, weakness, hard work and determination while the hagiographers glossed over his failings and presented him as a spiritual superman.

The vast majority of St Patrick's Day customs, myths and fables have been instituted and perpetuated since the hagiographies of Muirchú and Tírechán.

So, we have a choice to make. Do we believe Patrick himself or do we believe men with an agenda writing two hundred years later?

If we chose Patrick's own account then we lose the snake chasing, druid-destroying miracle man and the God versus the Devil power-plays. We also find no reference to the shamrock, and no naming of the mountain where Patrick tended animals as a slave.

Lough Derg is not mentioned, nor is Saul Church, Armagh Cathedral, nor the Paschal Fire on the Hill of Tara. In Patrick's own account, he was captured by slavers and tended sheep. In the later texts he was captured by the High King of Ireland and enslaved to Druids.

And, worst of all there is no mention whatsoever of green beer or corned beef and cabbage.

Instead, we discover a simple prayerful believer who spent more than 30 years faithfully proclaiming the gospel to the Irish people. We find a man full of the Holy Spirit who prophesied, dreamed, spoke in tongues and healed the sick. That's the sort of man I can relate to for I have been doing the same things myself for over forty years, as have thousands of other ordinary believers in Ireland.

Perhaps Peter was thinking of Hagiographic Spin Doctors when he wrote,

> For we did not follow cleverly devised
> stories or myths when we made known

to you the power and coming of our Lord Jesus Christ, but we were eyewitnesses of His majesty [His grandeur, His authority, His sovereignty].[2]

THE HOLY SPIRIT

UNDER THE OLD Covenant the Holy Spirit came upon the prophets when God wanted to speak to His people but the Holy Spirit did not live within the prophets. All this changed at Pentecost when the mantle of God's Spirit came upon His church and the third person of The Trinity came to live and dwell within believers.

Afterwards the indwelling Holy Spirit empowered and enabled His in-dwelt people to do His will. John said,

> But you have received the Holy Spirit, and he lives within you, so you don't need anyone to teach you what is true. For the Spirit teaches you everything you need to know, and what he teaches is true—it is not a lie. So just as he has

taught you, remain in fellowship with Christ.[1]

The everyday awareness of the indwelling power and communication of Holy Spirit was very important to Patrick. The gifts of the Holy Spirit were also commonplace in the Celtic Church, especially gifts of healings, prophecy and words of knowledge, alongside deliverance from demons.

Celtic Christians expected the gifts to function in the Church's life and ministry. That's a main reason why they left their old dumb gods.

St Patrick attributed his spiritual 'stamina' to the empowering of the Holy Spirit. In *The Confession* he said,

> He who wants can laugh and jeer, but I shall not keep silent nor keep hidden the signs and wonders which have been shown to me by the Lord before they took place as He who knows all things before the world began'.[2]

Patrick said these prophetic miraculous occurrences were accomplished by the power of the Holy Spirit. He wrote,

> Jesus' poured out on us abundantly His Holy Spirit, the gift and pledge of immortality, who makes those who

believe and obey to be sons of God and heirs along with Christ'.[3]

Patrick also attributes his prayer life to the work of Holy Spirit. He said, when first a slave in Ireland he was able to pray before dawn in all weathers, because the Spirit was fervent within him. Patrick also knew that baptism in the Holy Spirit, dreams, visions and prophecy were ongoing works of the Holy Spirit in everyday evangelism. He wrote,

> This Gospel of the kingdom shall be preached in the whole world for a testimony to all nations, and then shall come the end. And so too the Lord announces through the prophet, and says: And it shall come to pass, in the last days, saith the Lord, I will pour out of my Spirit upon all flesh; and your sons and your daughters shall prophesy, and your young men shall see visions, and your old men shall dream dreams. And upon my servants indeed, and upon my handmaids will I pour out in those days of my Spirit, and they shall prophesy.[4]

Patrick mentions a couple of dreams that involved speaking in tongues with interpretation. In one he heard

Jesus speaking words he could not understand until a voice gave an interpretation that filled Patrick with joy.

In the second dream Patrick saw the Holy Spirit inside him uttering unspeakable sighs, which couldn't be expressed in words. Their purpose was to strengthen Patrick.

Overall, Patrick's prayer life, mission and deep love of scripture was fuelled by the Holy Spirit.

When Patrick reflected on his long ministry in Ireland, he said he was protected from every evil because of God's Spirit dwelling within him.[5]

PATRICK'S SIMPLE STORY

THE SIMPLE STORY of Patrick's life in Ireland comes from his own writings. When he was sixteen, he was captured by Irish pirates from his home beyond Ireland and taken as a slave to Ireland where for six years he worked as an animal herder out in the open field in all weathers.

During this time Patrick repented of his unbelief and careless ways towards God and was converted and filled with the Holy Spirit. He wrote,

> The love of God and His fear came to me more and more, and my faith was strengthened. And my spirit was moved so that in a single day I would say as many as a hundred prayers, and almost as many in the night, and this even when I was staying in the woods

and on the mountains; and I used to get up for prayer before daylight, through snow, through frost, through rain, and I felt no harm, and there was no sloth in me, as I now see, because the spirit within me was then fervent.[1]

After six years God decided it was time to send Patrick back home to his family so he could become a priest in order to bring the Gospel of Jesus Christ back to the Irish.

Patrick also became a bishop but was hindered and opposed by other British bishops based on a sinful incident that happened in his teenage years.

With God's help, Patrick overcame this setback but was further challenged by others who questioned his motives for wishing to return to the Irish barbarians at the ends of the earth.

The Holy Spirit empowered Patrick to persevere and eventually have a fruitful ministry amongst the Irish who had previously enslaved him. Instead of tending sheep on the mountains he ended up tending thousands of God's sheep in the plains.

The eight dreams of St Patrick cover the period of his escape from Ireland, his call back to Ireland and the incident when he was opposed in his calling and ministry by the British bishops.

ST PATRICK'S EIGHT DREAMS

A QUARTER of St Patrick's biography concern dreams he personally experienced. Dreams were an important means of Patrick hearing God's voice. Perhaps he had hundreds, maybe thousands of dreams, and he only chose to tell us these few that best fitted his purpose for writing. I myself have been given many hundreds of dreams that have helped me in my ministry over the years.

Patrick valued and acted on his dreams. On one occasion he willingly risked his life by obeying a dream instruction that involved him walking 200 miles alone, through unknown bandit country.

I have recently written an 800 page book on all the dreams of the Bible and I find Patrick's dreams are very similar to biblical dreams in that their plain purpose is to implement God's plans and purpose upon the earth.

Dreams from God can be incredibility powerful

warheads released in the midst of life and death conflict and crisis. Like God's words in Jeremiah's mouth God's dreams can build up and plant or they can uproot, tear down, destroy and overthrow.[1]

Satan hates God's dreams because a successful interpretation and application of a God given dream always destroys his work. God's dreams are weapons of mass destruction that crush Satan's head.

God's dreams always advance and implement God's eternal plans and purpose. All history is a record of Sovereign Almighty God fulfilling His eternal plans and purpose and the created angel Satan failing to stop Him.

God sends dreams in order to advance His own Kingdom plans and purpose. The key word is purpose, not purposes and that purpose is Jesus Christ.

All of Patricks dreams advance the gospel of Jesus Christ even the one in which the devil attacked.

The eight dreams of St Patrick are,

- 1. **'You Have Fasted Well' Dream** - In this first dream Patrick heard a voice telling him he would soon return home.[2]
- 2. **'Your Ship Is Ready' Dream** - In this second dream, received a little later, Patrick heard a voice saying his ship of escape was ready.[3]
- 3. **'Satan Tested Patrick' Dream** – In this third dream Satan attacked Patrick but Christ the Lord delivered him.[4]

- 4. **'Two Months In Captivity' Dream** - In this fourth dream Patrick was captured when he received a divine message which accurately revealed the duration of his imprisonment stay.[5]
- 5. **'The Call Of the Irish' Dream** - In this fifth dream, received after he returned home, Patrick saw a night vision in which a man called Victoricus brought him countless letters from Ireland. As Patrick read the letters he could hear the voice of people with whom he had lived in Ireland pleading for his return.[6]
- 6. **'Jesus Speaks Within You' Dream** – In this sixth dream Patrick heard the authoritative voice of Jesus speaking but didn't understand what was said until it was interpreted.[7]
- 7. **'The Spirit Helps Our Weakness' Dream** – In this seventh dream Patrick experienced the Holy Spirit speaking within him and was awakened to two encouraging verses he remembered from the Bible.[8]
- 8. **'God's Displeasure Dream'** - In this eighth dream God assured Patrick of His constant protection and His disapproval of Patrick's accusers.[9]

HOW JESUS INTERPRETS DREAMS

Symbolic dreams are like parables. A parable is a type of metaphorical analogy requiring a proper interpretation before it releases its message.

The simple Christian definition is, a parable is an earthly story with a heavenly meaning. This definition also recognises the need for interpretation.

Jesus told parables and explained to His disciples how to interpret all parables. This occurs in Mark in *The Parable of the Sower,* which is like a complex symbolic dream. We have to read the whole passage but it will be worth while. The Bible says,

> Again Jesus began to teach by the lake. The crowd that gathered around him was so large that he got into a boat and sat in it out on the lake, while all the people were along the shore at the water's

edge. He taught them many things by parables, and in his teaching said: "Listen! A farmer went out to sow his seed. As he was scattering the seed, some fell along the path, and the birds came and ate it up. Some fell on rocky places, where it did not have much soil. It sprang up quickly, because the soil was shallow. But when the sun came up, the plants were scorched, and they withered because they had no root. Other seed fell among thorns, which grew up and choked the plants, so that they did not bear grain. Still other seed fell on good soil. It came up, grew and produced a crop, some multiplying thirty, some sixty, some a hundred times."

Then Jesus said, "Whoever has ears to hear, let them hear."

When he was alone, the Twelve and the others around him asked him about the parables. He told them, "The secret of the kingdom of God has been given to you. But to those on the outside everything is said in parables so that,

"'they may be ever seeing but never perceiving,
and ever hearing but never understanding;

otherwise they might turn and be forgiven!'"

Then Jesus said to them, "**Don't you understand this parable? How then will you understand any parable?** The farmer sows the word. Some people are like seed along the path, where the word is sown. As soon as they hear it, Satan comes and takes away the word that was sown in them. Others, like seed sown on rocky places, hear the word and at once receive it with joy. But since they have no root, they last only a short time. When trouble or persecution comes because of the word, they quickly fall away. Still others, like seed sown among thorns, hear the word; but the worries of this life, the deceitfulness of wealth and the desires for other things come in and choke the word, making it unfruitful. Others, like seed sown on good soil, hear the word, accept it, and produce a crop—some thirty, some sixty, some a hundred times what was sown."[1]

The method Jesus uses to interpret this parable can be called *The Symbol Replacement Method*. The main eight images in this parable are,

- The farmer
- The seed
- The birds
- The sun
- The roots
- The path without soil
- The rocky place with little soil
- The good soil

In Mark, Jesus replaced these symbols with other images that helped to unlock the true meaning of the parable.

- The farmer obviously represented a preacher. (Though Jesus doesn't say this.)
- The seed represented the word of God.
- The birds represented Satan and his demons.
- The sun represented trouble or persecution because of God's word,
- The roots represented the ability to survive and flourish.
- The path without soil represents no capacity to receive or nurture God's word.
- The rocky place with little soil represents people with shallow faith.
- The good soil represents people of spiritual depth and faith who reproduce themselves.

So instead of the parable being a story about a

farmer planting seed and facing difficulties it becomes a revelation of the process that occurs when a preacher or a prophet speaks the word of God. The world, the flesh and the devil all kick in and the hearer's hearts are tested.

Jesus said to his disciples, Don't you understand this parable? How then will you understand any parable? Here He was offering a key.

What He really meant was, **If you understand this parable then you will be able to understand all parables.**

All the dream interpreters in the Bible including the interpreting angels use *The Symbol Replacement Method* of dream interpretation.

For example, Pharaoh dreamed two dreams in quick succession. His first dream contained seven skinny cows that ate up seven fat cows, and his second dream contained seven thin heads of grain that ate up seven full heads of grain.

Using *The Symbol Replacement Method* Joseph interpreted the seven fat cows and the seven full heads of grain as seven years of abundant food production. Using the same method he then interpreted the seven skinny cows and the seven thin heads of grain as seven years of famine.

Consequently Joseph's interpretation of Pharaoh's dream was, Seven years of great abundance are coming throughout the land of Egypt, but seven years of famine will follow them.

For this interpretation Joseph was put in complete charge of the entire feeding program of the most powerful nation in the world. Not too difficult. Eh? Another good example comes from Daniel in Babylon. Scripture says God gave Daniel knowledge and understanding of all kinds of literature and learning and in understanding visions and dreams of all kinds.[2]

Let's take a look at Daniel interpreting, *Nebuchadnezzar's 'Large Statue' Dream*. Now this process was a little more difficult because Nebuchadnezzar wouldn't or couldn't tell Daniel the dream, and he was going to kill Daniel and others if they couldn't discover what his dream was and also interpret it. So Daniel had to get the dream from God and interpret it, which he did. Nebuchadnezzar's dream was,

> "Your Majesty looked, and there before you stood a large statue—an enormous, dazzling statue, awesome in appearance. The head of the statue was made of pure gold, its chest and arms of silver, its belly and thighs of bronze, its legs of iron, its feet partly of iron and partly of baked clay. While you were watching, a rock was cut out, but not by human hands. It struck the statue on its feet of iron and clay and smashed them. Then the iron, the clay, the bronze, the silver and the gold were all

broken to pieces and became like chaff on a threshing floor in the summer. The wind swept them away without leaving a trace. But the rock that struck the statue became a huge mountain and filled the whole earth.*³*

The symbols in this dream are,

- The large statue
- The head of gold
- The chest and arms of silver
- The belly and thighs of bronze
- The legs of iron
- The feet, partly of iron and partly of baked clay
- The rock not cut by human hands

When Daniel used *The Symbol Replacement Method*, these symbols were changed into what they represented.

- The large statue represented four kingdoms.
- The head of gold represented Nebuchadnezzar's kingdom.
- The chest and arms of silver represented an inferior kingdom.
- The belly and thighs of bronze represented another inferior kingdom.

- The legs of iron also represented another inferior kingdom.
- The feet, partly of iron and partly of baked clay represented disunity.
- The rock not cut by human hands represented Jesus' eternal kingdom

When Daniel used *The Symbol Replacement Method,* to interpret this dream he basically replaced each dream symbol with what it represented in reality.

Because of this Daniel could explain that Nebuchadnezzar was shown the successive kingdoms starting with his own kingdom, that God would use to rule over Israel until their Messiah would come.

With hindsight we now know, Nebuchadnezzar's dream spoke of four different empires - Babylon, Medo-Persia, Greece and Rome. Afterwards God would send His Messiah who'd establish His everlasting Kingdom.

The Scripture showing the *The Symbol Replacement Method,* in operation says,

> "This was the dream, and now we will interpret it to the king. Your Majesty, you are the king of kings. The God of heaven has given you dominion and power and might and glory; in your hands he has placed all mankind and the beasts of the field and the birds in the sky. Wherever they live, he has

made you ruler over them all. You are that head of gold.

"After you, another kingdom will arise, inferior to yours. Next, a third kingdom, one of bronze, will rule over the whole earth. Finally, there will be a fourth kingdom, strong as iron—for iron breaks and smashes everything—and as iron breaks things to pieces, so it will crush and break all the others. Just as you saw that the feet and toes were partly of baked clay and partly of iron, so this will be a divided kingdom; yet it will have some of the strength of iron in it, even as you saw iron mixed with clay. As the toes were partly iron and partly clay, so this kingdom will be partly strong and partly brittle. And just as you saw the iron mixed with baked clay, so the people will be a mixture and will not remain united, any more than iron mixes with clay.

"In the time of those kings, the God of heaven will set up a kingdom that will never be destroyed, nor will it be left to another people. It will crush all those kingdoms and bring them to an end, but it will itself endure forever. This is the meaning of the vision of the rock cut out of a mountain, but not by human hands—a rock that broke the iron, the bronze, the clay, the silver and the gold to pieces.

"The great God has shown the king what will take place in the future. The dream is true and its interpretation is trustworthy."*4*

It Is God Who Gives The Interpretation

Now all of that seems very simple, doesn't it? Well maybe not the bit about having to discover the contents of Nebuchadnezzar's dream otherwise you'll be killed.

So, before we begin to think it's as easy as painting by numbers I better mention something else. Both Joseph and Daniel understood this something else. Lets look at what they said about dream interpretation.

When Pharaoh's cupbearer and baker had dreams Joseph said, Do not interpretations belong to God? [5]

Later, Pharaoh said to Joseph, I had a dream, and no one can interpret it. But I have heard it said of you that when you hear a dream you can interpret it.

Joseph's truthful answer was, I cannot do it, but God will give Pharaoh the answer he desires.

Joseph was not being polite and self-effacing here. Although he intuitively understood *The Symbol Replace-*

ment Method he also knew it was only God who could give the proper interpretation.

The same thing happened with Daniel. When Nebuchadnezzar asked him, Are you able to tell me what I saw in my dream and interpret it, Daniel honestly replied,

> No wise man, enchanter, magician or diviner can explain to the king the mystery he has asked about, but there is a God in heaven who reveals mysteries. He has shown King Nebuchadnezzar what will happen in days to come. [6]

Daniel also told Nebuchadnezzar,

> The revealer of mysteries showed you what is going to happen. As for me, this mystery has been revealed to me, not because I have greater wisdom than anyone else alive, but so that Your Majesty may know the interpretation and that you may understand what went through your mind.[7]

Like Joseph, Daniel was not being polite and self-effacing. Although Daniel intuitively understood the *Symbol Replacement Method* he also knew it was only God who could give the proper dream interpretation.

But what about the pagan Midianite's dream?

Good question, because the soldier's friend also interpreted *The Midianite's Dream for Gideon* using the *Symbol Replacement Method*. The Bible says,

> Gideon arrived just as a man was telling a friend his dream. "I had a dream," he was saying. "A round loaf of barley bread came tumbling into the Midianite camp. It struck the tent with such force that the tent overturned and collapsed."
>
> His friend responded, "This can be nothing other than the sword of Gideon son of Joash, the Israelite. God has given the Midianites and the whole camp into his hands."[8]

The symbols in this dream are,

- A round loaf of barley bread
- The Midianite camp
- A tent

When the friend used *The Symbol Replacement Method*, these symbols changed into what they represented in reality.

- The round loaf of barley bread represented Gideon's sword of power and his small army.
- The Midianite camp represented the Midianite army
  - The tent represented the protective covering and place of rest for the Midianite soldiers.

The soldier's friend understood these symbols and was able to declare God's truth that Gideon's small army would be victorious over the vastly superior Midianite army.

NOTES ON PATRICK'S DREAMS

FOUR OF PATRICK'S dreams are literal and easily understood. The other four are symbolic and require interpretation. Three of the dreams concern the indwelling of God's Holy Spirit and involve speaking in tongues.

The indwelling ministry of the Holy Spirit allows Jesus to dwell in a believer's heart forever. In this way God works in a Christian's life, helping them conform to the character of Christ. Paul mentioned this in Romans. He said,

> For those whom he foreknew he also predestined to be conformed to the image of his Son, in order that he might be the firstborn among many brothers.[1]

Literal or Symbolic?

1. 'You Have Fasted Well' Dream - In this first dream Patrick heard a voice telling him he would soon return to Britain.[2] This is a **literal** dream with a voice speaking.

2. 'Your Ship Is Ready' Dream - In this second dream, Patrick heard a voice saying his ship of escape was ready.[3] This is a literal dream with a voice speaking. There also seems to be a visual portion because Patrick was told to look. Perhaps he was shown the location of the harbour two hundred miles away.

3. 'Satan Tested Patrick' Dream – In this third dream Satan attacked Patrick but Christ delivered him.[4] This is a symbolic dream with a heavy rock, the sun, and an unknown word, Helias, that needs interpreted. Patrick speaks out this word given by the Holy Spirit. Afterwards Patrick said, I believe I was helped by Christ the Lord, and that his Spirit cried out for me. This is typical tongues and interpretation in operation.

4. 'Two Months In Captivity' Dream - In this fourth dream Patrick was captured when he received a divine message which accurately revealed the duration of his captivity.[5] This is a literal dream with a voice speaking.

5. **'The Call Of the Irish' Dream** - In this fifth dream, received after he returned home, Patrick saw a man called Victoricus who brought him letters from Ireland. As Patrick read the letters he could hear the voice of people amongst whom he had lived in Ireland pleading for his return.[6] This is a symbolic dream with an unknown man called Victorious, numerous letters, one of which said, the voice of the Irish.

6. **'Jesus Speaks Within You' Dream** – In this sixth dream Patrick heard the authoritative voice of Jesus speaking but didn't understand what was said until it was interpreted.[7] This is a symbolic dream with a voice talking that is interpreted as Jesus speaking.

7. **'The Spirit Helps Our Weakness' Dream** – In this seventh dream Patrick experienced the Holy Spirit speaking within him and was awakened to two encouraging Bible verses that interpreted the dream experience.[8] This is a symbolic dream in which Patrick finds himself inside his own body.

8. **'God's Displeasure Dream'** - In this eighth dream God assured Patrick of His constant protection and His disapproval of Patrick's accusers.[9] This is a literal dream

with a symbolic aspect. There is writing we're not told the meaning of, and a scripture that interprets the dream.

Dreams - As Answers to Prayer

St Patrick uses two different phrases when talking about his dreams. In the four dreams where he sees things - seer's dreams - he uses the biblical phrase, a vision of the night.[10]

In the other four dreams he introduces the dream narrative with the phrase 'responsum divinum'.[11] This indicates God sent these dreams in response to Patrick's prayers.

The four dreams where he uses the phrase a vision of the night, are *Satan Tested Patrick Dream, The Call of The Irish Dream, Jesus Speaks Within You Dream* and *The Spirit Helps Our Weakness Dream.*

In the *Satan Tested Patrick Dream,* Satan physically attacked Patrick who was delivered by Christ the Lord, when His spirit cried out for Patrick.

In the *The Call of The Irish Dream,* God gave Patrick a symbolic calling dream in which he heard the voice of the Irish saying, We beg you, holy boy, to come and walk again among us.

In the *Jesus Speaks Within You Dream,* Patrick heard Jesus praying in a language he couldn't understand until it was interpreted as, The one who gave his life for you, he it is who speaks in you. Patrick then awoke full of joy.

In *The Spirit Helps Our Weakness Dream*, Patrick was amazed and astonished at the Holy Spirit praying within him. He was reminded of the scripture that says, The Spirit helps the weaknesses of our prayer; for we do know what it is we should pray.[12]

The Answer to Prayer Dreams

The four dreams where 'responsum divinum' is used are the, *You Have Fasted Well Dream, Your Ship Is Ready Dream, Two Months In Captivity Dream* and *God's Displeasure Dream*.

In the You Have Fasted Well Dream, Patrick must have been praying and fasting in order to escape from slavery when he received the dream message that said, You have fasted well. Very soon you will return to your native country.

In the Your Ship Is Ready Dream, Patrick must have been praying about the timing and place of escape, when the dream voice said. Look – your ship is ready, and he was shown where to go to.

In the Two Months In Captivity Dream, Patrick must have been praying and asking God about how long he would be held captive when God responded by sending a dream in which Patrick heard the divine answer, You will be with them for two months.

In the God's Displeasure Dream, Patrick must have been praying about the unfair accusations being levelled against him when God sent a dream in which He said, We have seen with displeasure the face of the one who was chosen deprived of his good name. God also assured Patrick, He who touches you as it were touches the pupil of my eye.[13]

Bible Dreams That Answered Prayer

Of the fifty four Bible dreams I studied for my book *All God's Bible Dreams* there were only a couple that were given in answer to prayer.

In Genesis, God had promised land to Abraham, but Abraham was getting impatient. He said, Sovereign Lord, how can I know that I will gain possession of it? In answer, God sent a dream I call *Abraham's Covenant Dream.*

In the Book of Daniel, God sent a dream to the pagan King Nebuchadnezzar. This king had commanded his wise men and dream interpreters to do a miraculous thing. They had to discover what he had actually dreamed and interpret it otherwise the king would have them killed.

Daniel and his friends Hananiah, Mishael and Azariah prayed for mercy from God and God revealed the contents of Nebuchadnezzar's dream and its interpretation in a dream to Daniel, thereby saving their lives.

All Patrick's Dreams Concern Prayer

All of Patrick's eight dreams concern prayer. The first four 'responsum divinum' dreams, *You Have Fasted Well Dream, Your Ship Is Ready Dream, Two Months In Captivity Dream* and *God's Displeasure Dream,* were given in response to prayer.

In the *Satan Tested Patrick Dream,* Patrick believed the spirit of Christ the Lord cried out in prayer for him.

In the *The Call of The Irish Dream,* it is the Irish themselves who are praying that Patrick will come back to them. Patrick says, Thanks be to God, after many years the Lord granted them what they were calling for.

In the *Jesus Speaks Within You Dream,* Jesus was doing the praying.

In *The Spirit Helps Our Weakness Dream,* the Holy Spirit was praying.

God Sovereignty

God's sovereignty is rarely mentioned nowadays in Christian circles and never in secular society. Yet we need some grasp of the reality of God's sovereignty in order to correctly understand God's dreams because every Bible dream and every dream of St Patrick, was sent to fulfil a specific sovereign plan and purpose of God.

Understanding God's purpose is a major key to unlocking God's dreams. The Sovereignty of God is the biblical teaching that all things are under God's rule and control, and nothing happens without His direction or His permission.

This means God works not just some things but all things according to His will.[14] Throughout scripture Yahweh is revealed as the One True God who governs and directs all things for His Chosen People.

There's never a sense of God being a cosmic clockmaker who leaves human beings to their own devices. Instead, He is shown as actively intervening and interfering in human affairs, sometimes through dreams, in order to advance His kingdom plans and purpose.

As regards the 54 Bible dreams I examined in my book called, *All God's Bible Dreams*, the statistics are,

- In 62 % of them God demonstrated His sovereign dominion over all the powers and principalities attacking His Covenant People and their seed line.
- In 26% of them God encouraged and guided His Covenant People with specific direction for their well-being and the safety of their seed line.

- In 8% of Bible dreams God prevented kings and leaders from harming His Covenant People and their seed line, and instead He caused them to bless His people.
- In the remaining 4% of Bible dreams God helped and encouraged His New Testament Covenant People to carry out the Great Commission of Jesus Christ.

All Bible dreams are connected in one way or another with Jesus Christ. They are mostly about keeping Jesus' seed line pure and safe so He could be born. The rest of the dreams are to do with spreading His Good News.

All of Patrick's dreams are about equipping him, protecting him and strengthening him to preach the gospel of Jesus Christ to the pagan Irish so that Jesus should see the travail of His soul and be satisfied.[15]

The Indwelling Holy Spirit

St Patrick had a strong awareness of the indwelling Holy Spirit of God. This is seen in three of his dreams.

The indwelling of the Holy Spirit refers to God taking up permanent residence in the body of a believer in Jesus Christ. In the Old Testament, the Spirit would come and go from the believers, empowering them for service but not necessarily remaining with them.

Jesus in the New Testament, on the other hand, told His disciples, He lives with you and will be in you.[16] He also said,

> Anyone who loves me will obey my teaching. My Father will love them, and we will come to them and make our home with them.[17]

Later Paul wrote,

> Do you not know that your bodies are temples of the Holy Spirit, who is in you, whom you have received from God?[18]

In the *Satan Tested Patrick Dream,* when Satan was attacking Patrick, it was the Spirit of Christ the Lord that cried out for him. Patrick realised this and quoted from Matthew who said,

> In that day, the Lord testifies, it will not be you who will speak, but the Spirit of your Father who speaks in you.[19]

Another translation says,

> For it is not you who will be speaking—it

will be the Spirit of your Father speaking through you.[20]

In the *Jesus Speaks Within You Dream* Patrick heard authoritative words he couldn't understand. He didn't know if the words were coming from within him or outside of him. In the end when the words are translated, he realised it was Jesus who was speaking from inside him. Then he awoke full of joy.

In *The Spirit Helps Our Weakness Dream* Patrick felt as if he was within his own body and the Holy Spirit was interceding with deep sighs over him and also within Patrick's body.

The Holy Spirit then brought two scriptures to Patrick's mind. One said,

> The Spirit helps the weaknesses of our prayer; for we do know what it is we should pray, but the very Spirit pleads for us with unspeakable sighs, which cannot be expressed in word.[21]

The other said,

> The Lord is our advocate, and pleads for us.[22]

The New International Version says,

But the Advocate, the Holy Spirit, whom the Father will send in my name, will teach you all things and will remind you of everything I have said to you. Peace I leave with you; my peace I give you. I do not give to you as the world gives. Do not let your hearts be troubled and do not be afraid.[23]

PRAYING IN TONGUES DREAMS

THE GREATEST GIFT God ever gave to mankind was Jesus. The greatest gift Jesus ever gave to His Church was the Holy Spirit and the greatest gift the Holy Spirit ever gave to a believer was the gift of praying in tongues.

The gift is sometimes called speaking in tongues. It has also been termed the gift of our own spirit language.

When Paul writes about people who speak in tongues, he is referring to a Spirit-led activity in which a believer in Jesus praises and communicates with God by speaking in a language they have never learned.

Today around 700 million Christians speak in tongues, and it's reckoned 95% of them aren't fully aware of the enormous spiritual benefits.

Basically, there are three manifestations of the gift of praying in tongues and each expression serves a different purpose. These have been helpfully termed,

The Proof Tongue, The Prophetic Tongue, and *The Personal Tongue.*

God mainly has a specific purpose for each of these categories, but we can't put God in a box. All three categories can function at any time in any situation at God' discretion, depending on His purpose.

As we briefly look at each manifestation, we should keep in mind that Patrick's three dreams regarding tongues concern *The Personal Tongue* with interpretation.

1. The Proof Tongue - God's purpose for the proof tongue is as a sign and a potential benefit for unbelievers. The proof tongue is supernaturally understood by the unbeliever and doesn't require and interpreter. We see this occurring in *The Book of Acts* when God-fearing Jews from every nation under heaven heard and understood the disciples, including Jesus' mother Mary, speaking in tongues.

These Jews knew nothing about Jesus as the Messiah, until the phenomena of speaking in tongues caused them to be amazed and perplexed and ask questions. Afterwards three thousand of them became believers in Jesus through Peter's preaching.

2. The Prophetic Tongue – God's purpose for the prophetic tongue is that it should be spoken loudly and interpreted in the midst of a gathering of believers so they may be strengthened by its prophetic content. The prophetic tongue always requires an interpreter.[1]

Paul saw tongues as a normal part of church life. He said, When you come together, each of you has a hymn, or a word of instruction, a revelation, a tongue or an interpretation. Everything must be done so that the church may be built up.

He also helpfully clarified that if there was no interpreter of tongues present that particular day the speaker should keep quiet and speak only to himself and to God.

Speaking in tongues in church without an interpretation doesn't help anyone. In fact, it might confuse unbelievers.[2]

3. The Personal Tongue – God's purpose for the personal tongue is to edify and strengthen the individual believer. The personal tongue doesn't necessarily need an interpretation in order to bless the individual, but an interpretation will greatly increase its impact.

That's one of the reasons Paul encourages believers who speak in tongues to pray for the ability to interpret.[3]

Paul who spoke in tongues more than any other believer and who wrote half of the New Testament functioned in tongues and interpretation.

The personal tongue is mainly for self-edification, and it's usually a heavenly language though I've been at a meeting where a group of Iranians understood the tongues of a young Irish Christian who had no knowledge whatsoever of the Iranian language.

Speaking in tongues enables believers to say prayers that are in total agreement with the will of God because the Holy Spirit both gives and directs their prayers. Perhaps the only time we can ever be 100% certain sure that our prayers are in the complete will of God is when we are speaking in tongues. No wonder Satan hates it so much. John says,

> This is the confidence we have in approaching God: that if we ask anything according to his will, he hears us. And if we know that he hears us—whatever we ask—we know that we have what we asked of him.[4]

Paul in Romans says the Holy Spirit makes intercession for all believers according to the will of God. He also says the Holy Spirit searches the heart of a man or a woman and knows their needs and desires, and also God's will concerning those needs and desires.[5]

Prayer is the life blood of God's Kingdom and God always seeks for those who'll intercede for His sovereign will to be done on earth as it is in heaven. Ezekiel highlights this,

> I looked for someone among them who would build up the wall and stand

before me in the gap on behalf of the land so I would not have to destroy it, but I found no one.[6]

Jesus told His disciples to pray God would raise up suitable workers for the world's harvest fields, including Ireland. He said,

> The harvest is great, but the workers are few. So pray to the Lord who is in charge of the harvest; ask him to send more workers into his fields.[7]

God sent Patrick into the fertile harvest field of Ireland as an apostle who preached the gospel and planted churches.

Patrick was a strong intercessor, even from his early days as a slave. He was a man who built up the church and stood in the gap before God on behalf of the Irish nation.

As mentioned in the previous chapter four of Patrick's dreams were sent in response to prayer. These were the, *You Have Fasted Well Dream, Your Ship Is Ready Dream, Two Months In Captivity Dream,* and *God's Displeasure Dream.* These were all simple literal dreams.

The remaining four symbolic dreams also concerned prayer. In one dream the Irish are praying for Patrick's return. In another Patrick was crying out in prayer for deliverance from Satan. In the two remaining dreams, the Spirit of Christ and the Holy Spirit were interceding for Patrick.

Three of these symbolic dreams also involved the spiritual gift of speaking tongues. All three dreams were to do with life in the Holy Spirit and symbolically displayed Jesus' promise concerning the Promised Holy Spirit as recorded in John 14,

> If you love me, keep my commands. And I will ask the Father, and he will give you another advocate to help you and be with you forever— the Spirit of truth. The world cannot accept him, because it neither sees him nor knows him. But you know him, for he lives with you and will be in you. I will not leave you as orphans; I will come to you.
> Before long, the world will not see me anymore, but you will see me. Because I live, you also will live. On that day you will realise that I am in my Father, and you are in me, and I am in you. Whoever has my commands and keeps them is the one who loves me. The one who loves me will be loved by my Father, and I too will love them and show myself to them.[8]

Jesus spoke about the indwelling Holy Spirit. He said,

> On that day you will realise that I am in my Father, and you are in me, and I am in you.[9]

Humanly speaking, this is not an easy concept to visualise or comprehend. Imagine stopping a stranger on the street and telling them that Jesus is in God the Father, and you are in Jesus and Jesus is in you.

How do you think they might respond? Might they play along with your thinking? Might they ask, Does that mean God is in you and you are in God? Might they ask also where the Holy Spirit is?

In all three of Patrick's 'Life in the Spirit' or 'Speaking in Tongues' dreams we see a symbolic representation of how this 'You in Me' - indwelling Holy Spirit reality functions in practice.

In each of Patrick's eight dreams there is always a voice speaking and I believe in seven of the dreams that voice belongs to God or one of the Trinity.

- In dreams 1, 2 and 4 it is called a divine voice. These three literal dreams need no interpretation.
- In dream 3 the Holy Spirit speaks, and Patrick gives the interpretation.

- In dream five it is the voice of the Irish speaking and Patrick interprets it as a call to return to Ireland.
- In dream 6 Jesus speaks and also interprets.
- In dream 7 the Holy Spirit speaks, and Patrick interprets.
- In dream 8 the Trinity speaks, and Patrick brings an interpretation.
- In five of his eight dreams Patrick is involved in the interpretative process.

We will look at these things in more detail when we look at each specific dream.

SIX SOURCES OF DREAMS

THERE ARE four kinds of dreams mentioned in Scripture and two other kinds that came into play after the Holy Spirit was poured out at Pentecost.

It's important to know that God's always sends a dream appropriate to the dreamer's metron. Metron is a greek word that refers to the dreamer's level of authority and sphere of influence. God always sends His dream to a credible person who is in a position to either share the dream or implement the dream's instruction.

For example, Pharaoh's Cupbearer was totally unable to promote Joseph to a high position in Egypt but his metron allowed him to introduce Joseph to Pharaoh who did in fact have the metron to promote Joseph to the position God had intended for him.

- Firstly, there are *True Dreams* that are direct messages from God. These comprise 96% of all the recorded dreams in the Bible.
- Secondly, there are *Satanic Dreams*. There are only three mentioned, and two examples of such dreams in Scripture.
- Thirdly there are *False Dreams* which are made-up delusions from the evil hearts and minds of men. We have no actual example of one of these dreams though God warns us about them.
- Fourthly there are *Natural Dreams* that arise from the dreamer's personal self. We have scriptures speaking about these dreams but no actual recorded examples.
- Fifthly there are *Believer's Dreams* that arise from the renewed spirits of Christians. We have no mention or actual example of these dreams in the Bible.
- Sixthly there are *Unbeliever's Dreams* that arise from the hearts of unsaved human beings. There are no recorded examples of these dreams in the Bible.

God's True Dreams

God sends dreams in order to advance His own Kingdom plans and purpose. The key word is purpose, not purposes and that purpose is Jesus Christ.

Five of Patrick's eight dreams are from God. Their purpose was to guide and encourage Patrick into his ministry of being an apostolic evangelist who preached the life giving word of God. One of Patrick's dreams enabled him to escape from captivity in Ireland. Years later another dream called him back to Ireland as a missionary. Patrick's dreams also encouraged and edified him when he was in the mission field under pressure.

Satanic Dreams

Satan hates God's dreams because a successful interpretation and application of a God given dream always destroys his work. God's dreams crush Satan's head.

In the Bible, Eliphaz and Job were assailed by demonic dreams and nightmares. Although we know nothing about the actual content of Job's dreams we do know the purpose was to break Job's trust in God.

In Eliphaz's dream Satan used half truths to confuse Eliphaz. Eliphaz wrongly believed the dream was from God and quoted it as such. Eliphaz wasn't able to overcome the evil spirit by quoting God's word.

In *All God's Bible Dreams*, I also consider the possibility that Jesus being tempted by Satan was a dream. In the *Jesus' Tempted By Satan Dream*, Jesus completely defeated Satan by quoting the word of God.

In Patrick's *Satan Tested Patrick Dream*, Satan physically attacks Patrick but Patrick calls out in distress and is delivered by Christ the Lord, whose Spirit cried out for Patrick.

False Dreams

Jeremiah said false dreams are from deceitful prophets who have not stood in God's presence and who've not been sent by Him. God calls them, lying prophets, who prophesy the delusions of their own minds.[1]

God tells His people not to listen to the made up dreams of these false prophets and mediums who try to fool God's people by prophesying lies in God's name.[2] The purpose of these false dreamers is to lead God's people into sin and away from God's plans and purpose.[3] Moses also warns about this,

> If a prophet, or one who foretells by
>   dreams, appears among you and
>   announces to you a sign or wonder,
>   and if the sign or wonder spoken of
>   takes place, and the prophet says, "Let
>   us follow other gods" (gods you have
>   not known) "and let us worship them,"
>   you must not listen to the words of that
>   prophet or dreamer.
> The Lord your God is testing you to find
>   out whether you love him with all your

heart and with all your soul. It is the Lord your God you must follow, and him you must revere. Keep his commands and obey him; serve him and hold fast to him.

That prophet or dreamer must be put to death for inciting rebellion against the Lord your God, who brought you out of Egypt and redeemed you from the land of slavery. That prophet or dreamer tried to turn you from the way the Lord your God commanded you to follow. You must purge the evil from among you.[4]

Joseph Smith who generated Mormonism and Muhammad who generated Islam all had dreams that led people away from a proper understanding and worship of Jesus as God.

Jeremiah also said God wants His true prophets to recount their dreams faithfully because their powerful dreams from Him will be like fire and a hammer that breaks a rock in pieces.[5]

The false prophets on the other hand steal words from one another and imagine fake dreams. Concerning these dreamers, God says,

> Indeed, I am against those who prophesy false dreams," declares the Lord. "They

tell them and lead my people astray with their reckless lies, yet I did not send or appoint them. They do not benefit these people in the least," declares the Lord.[6]

In the New Testament, Jude also warns against false dreamers who defile their bodies, reject authority, and slander glorious beings.[7] Their evil dreams are not from God but from their own imaginations and sinful hearts.

There are no false dreams in St Patrick's writings.

Natural Dreams

God's purposes for sleep and dreams not only concern spiritual revelation. The vast majority of our dreams are from our natural selves. We have scriptures speaking about these dreams but no actual recorded examples. Nowadays we tend to identify these dreams with labels like *Processing Dreams* or *Soul Dreams.*

Soul Dreams seem to be processing dreams that have some sense of meaning to them. These dreams can often be interpreted. They tend to deal with suppressed emotions, attitudes, beliefs and issues we need to bring to the surface and bring to the Lord. They may refer to our past, present or even our concerns for the future.

Soul dreams often provide us with new insights into our inner world and occasionally they may even offer solutions for difficult personal problems. Soul dreams usually flag up issues that are best shared with pastors or other wise believers. They can often help us process these dreams and achieve a spiritual breakthrough in some relevant area.

These *Processing Dreams* are vital for good mental and emotional health. These God given REM dreams nightly recalibrate and fine-tune the emotional circuits of our brains. Proper sleep and dreaming resets and benefits our mental and physical health.

These dreams also show God's loving care because sleeping and dreaming are just as important for our lives as eating, drinking and breathing. The quality of our sleeping and dreaming is as vital to our well-being as the quality of our food, drink and air. The better the quality the better the life.

Dreaming is now being called 'overnight therapy' by some neuroscientists. Recent research discovered a major benefit of dreaming is in processing our daily emotional experiences so we can make sense of conflicting issues and move on with our lives.

Because we are daily faced with difficult issues, anxiety dreams are very common. They are usually triggered by internal stressors like angry emotions and impulses or external stressors like past trauma, a bad day at work, or an anxious response to whatever current crisis the media is throwing at us.

These dreams can be about past events, repressed desires, and unfulfilled hopes. Wish fulfilment dreams about possible marriage partners fall into this category.

Isaiah likens such fleeting dreams to a hungry person who dreams of eating but wakens up still hungry and a thirsty person who dreams of drinking but wakens up faint and thirsty.[8]

Perhaps Solomon sums it up best when he says, Too much activity gives you restless dreams.[9] There are no natural dreams in St Patrick's writings.

Believer's Dreams

Spiritually, there's a vast difference between a believer's dream and an unbeliever's dream. Various words have been used to describe a believer's salvation experience including, born again, renewed, saving faith, and regenerated. When I use the word believer, I'm referring to such a person. All true believers are indwelled by the Holy Spirit. Jesus said,

> Anyone who loves me will obey my teaching. My Father will love them, and we will come to them and make our home with them. Anyone who does not love me will not obey my teaching. These words you hear are not my own; they belong to the Father who sent me.[10]

Paul describes the indwelling experience of the Holy Spirit as the believer being joined unto the Lord in one spirit. The image is of an inseparable union.[11]

Because of this profound union it's not always easy to tell whether a dream is from the Holy Spirit or from the believer's human spirit. Yet the Holy Spirit's activity is always evident in both situations and the final purpose is always the same, which is to equip and enable the believer to fulfil his life's purpose and do the will of God.

Dreams from a believer's spirit tend to be similar to personal prophecy. They often confirm words God has already spoken and like prophecy they tend to strengthen, encourage, and comfort the believer.[12]

Jesus told his disciples,

> The Comforter, which is the Holy Ghost, whom the Father will send in my name, he shall teach you all things, and bring all things to your remembrance, whatsoever I have said unto you.[13]

A major part of the Holy Spirit's comforting role is to help us in our daily lives as we grown up from being spiritual babies drinking milk into mature believers who are able to feed ourselves on the meat of God's word.[14]

We're all at various stages and we all have different callings, anointings and metrons. God understands this and the Holy Spirit, like a mother who never forgets her suckling child,[15] constantly identifies with our growing pains and struggles in life and regularly reassures and motivates us through prophecy, dreams and visions. The work of encouraging and strengthening the saints is an ongoing work of the Holy Spirit and of all believers. Paul told the saints in Thessalonica to encourage and build one another up.[16]

Both the Holy Spirit and our own renewed spirit can give us supernatural dreams in order to teach, guide, guard, correct, renew, encourage, and enlighten us in our daily walk with God. Often these dreams counteract the constant bombardment of the world, the flesh and the devil.

God's desire for the believer's spirit is to daily grow in heavenly wisdom, revelation, understanding and power. Paul said,

> I keep asking that the God of our Lord
> Jesus Christ, the glorious Father, may
> give you the Spirit of wisdom and reve-
> lation, so that you may know him
> better. I pray that the eyes of your
> heart may be enlightened in order that
> you may know the hope to which he
> has called you, the riches of his glorious
> inheritance in his holy people, and his
> incomparably great power for us who
> believe.[17]

Scripture also says our renewed spirit works with the Holy Spirit and searches the inner depths of our hearts and minds. Proverbs says, The spirit of man is the lamp of the Lord, searching all his innermost parts[18] and Paul similarly says, For who among men knows the thoughts of a man except the man's spirit within him?[19] One of the ways the result of this spiritual searching is manifested to our conscious mind is through dreams.

The simple rule and general consensus is that dreams from God tend to have more authority and are more commanding while dreams from our renewed human spirit tend to be more suggestive and confirming.

For example, a dream from God might tell the dreamer to go to a certain nation to minister while a dream from a renewed human spirit might show the dreamer that God loves them and will never leave them.

A dream from God might tell a mature Christian dreamer how to raise £10 million for an international outreach programme while a renewed spirit dream might strengthen the dreamer by consoling them their prayers have been heard and will be answered.

This delicate skill of knowing whether a revelation is from God or our renewed spirit can be seen in Paul's writing. When he was speaking to the Corinthians about marriage issues Paul said,

> To the married I give this command (not I, but the Lord): A wife must not separate from her husband. But if she does, she must remain unmarried or else be reconciled to her husband. And a

husband must not divorce his wife. To the rest I say this (I, not the Lord): If any brother has a wife who is not a believer and she is willing to live with him, he must not divorce her.[20]

Here Paul makes a clear distinction between what he knows is from the Holy Spirit and what he knows is from his own renewed spirit and he gives the greater weight of authority to God's leading. Yet he also trusts the discernment of his own spirit.

Later in the same chapter Paul again deals with another subtle issue. He says,

A woman is bound to her husband as long as he lives. But if her husband dies, she is free to marry anyone she wishes, but he must belong to the Lord. In my judgment, she is happier if she stays as she is—and I think that I too have the Spirit of God.[21]

In these verses, Paul makes a distinction between God's command to marry someone who belongs to the Lord and his personal judgement the widow would be happier if she didn't marry at all in the prevailing circumstances.

Paul also adds the comment that he feels God agrees

with him, but he understands this revelation from his own spirit is not binding on the widow.

Like Paul, the more we grow in the wisdom and revelation of God and His power the more our renewed spirit can impact and influence our daily thinking. This Godly impact of our renewed spirit upon our thinking often manifests in dreams.

My sense is that most of the dreams a Christian dream interpreter encounters from believers are of this renewed spirit type, alongside some natural dreams. Normally as Christians grow in their understanding of dreams they tend to better understand the source of their dreams and consequently don't require an interpreter's help to the same extent.

Patrick had two believer's dreams from his renewed spirit.

Unbeliever's Dreams

There's a world of difference between a believer's dream and an unbeliever's dream both in content and purpose. The believer is one spirit with the Lord. He walks in the light and loves and obeys God. The unbeliever on the other hand walks in darkness under the jurisdiction of Satan and cannot love or obey God.

Jesus said,

> Anyone who loves me will obey my teaching. My Father will love them, and we

will come to them and make our home with them. Anyone who does not love me will not obey my teaching. These words you hear are not my own; they belong to the Father who sent me.[22]

Dreams from God or the believer's renewed spirit will bring enlightenment, healing, renewal, correction, and guidance into our lives. On the other hand, dreams arising from an unrenewed person will tend to cause anxiety, confusion, discouragement, fear, distortion, deception, and falsehood. Their purpose is to hinder the unbeliever from finding God's plans and purposes for their lives. Paul alludes to this,

> But the natural [unbelieving] man does not accept the things [the teachings and revelations] of the Spirit of God, for they are foolishness [absurd and illogical] to him; and he is incapable of understanding them, because they are spiritually discerned and appreciated, [and he is unqualified to judge spiritual matters].[23]

James writes about two kinds of wisdom in his letter. He says,

> Who is wise and understanding among

you? Let them show it by their good life, by deeds done in the humility that comes from wisdom. But if you harbour bitter envy and selfish ambition in your hearts, do not boast about it or deny the truth. Such "wisdom" does not come down from heaven but is earthly, unspiritual, demonic. For where you have envy and selfish ambition, there you find disorder and every evil practice. But the wisdom that comes from heaven is first of all pure; then peace-loving, considerate, submissive, full of mercy and good fruit, impartial and sincere. Peacemakers who sow in peace reap a harvest of righteousness.*24*

Dreams from God or from a believer's renewed spirit are wisdom from above. They will be first of all pure; then peace-loving, considerate, submissive, full of mercy and good fruit, impartial and sincere. They will encourage the believer to do God's will.[25]

Dreams from Satan or from an unbeliever's spirit on the other hand are earthly, soulish, and demonic.[26]. Earthly dreams are full of the cares of this world that preoccupy the dreamer's thoughts.[27] Soulish dreams also fill the dreamer's mind with lust and sensual longings, selfish ambitions, unfulfilled assumptions, expectations and multifarious kinds of illusions and vain thinking. Think internet!

Demonic dreams are jam packed with fear and lies. They are typically full of fantasies that appeal to the unbeliever's illusions of pride. Their purpose is to confuse and create condemnation in order to keep the dreamer from seeking God and His plans and purpose for their lives.

Paul warns the believers at Ephesus against such thinking. He said,

> I tell you this, and insist on it in the Lord, that you must no longer live as the Gentiles do, in the futility of their thinking. They are darkened in their understanding and separated from the life of God because of the ignorance that is in them due to the hardening of their hearts. Having lost all sensitivity, they have given themselves over to sensuality so as to indulge in every kind of impurity, and they are full of greed.[28]

Believers who set their minds and desires on earthly things and not on higher spiritual things from above can also be badly troubled by disturbing fleshly dreams.[29]

There are no unbeliever's dreams in Patrick's writing.

DREAM INTERPRETER PATRICK

THE MAJORITY of Bible dreams are literal and easily understood. Twenty nine of the Bible's fifty four dreams are literal.

God isn't in the business of sending riddles and puzzles just to confuse or amuse people.

Whenever God sent a complicated symbolic Bible dream, He always made sure there was a dream interpreter on hand.

Four of Patrick's eight dreams are symbolic and Patrick was able to correctly record and interpret them.

This makes Patrick a dream interpreter.

I believe dream interpretation was one of the gifts Patrick regularly functioned in alongside teaching, preaching, healings, miracles, and prophecy.

I think of Arthur O'Shaughnessy's Ode concerning the Irish,

> We are the music makers,
>   And we are the dreamers of dreams,
> Wandering by lone sea-breakers,
>   And sitting by desolate streams; —
> World-losers and world-forsakers,
>   On whom the pale moon gleams:
> Yet we are the movers and shakers
>   Of the world for ever, it seems.

Wouldn't it have been wonderful listening to Patrick interpret dreams for the spiritually hungry Irish?

UNDER THE MICROSCOPE

In the next section I want to put St Patrick's eight dreams under the microscope. I'll do this using a personal checklist I created based on Paul's prayer for the Ephesians.[1]

This section changes from a narrative genre to a teaching role. A main purpose for me is to show Christian dream interpreters how I interpret Patrick's dreams using my Biblical worldview. That's why I switch to this new teaching structure. Please bear with me and enjoy!

This checklist provides a consistency and an accountability to the interpretative process. It helps stop me cutting corners and it gives me a better overall interpretation and perspective.

All Bible dreams concern Jesus in one way or another and the three main characters are always God, Satan and the dreamer.

There are only three types of spiritual beings and

three sources of spiritual activity. There is God and His faithful spirits who are always good and holy. There is Satan and his rebellious spirits who are always bad and evil.

Then there is humanity whose spirit is either good or bad based on whether they are being influenced and ruled by God's Holy Spirit or Satan's evil spirit.

Let me again state a truth. God's dreams always advance and implement God's eternal plans and purpose. All history is a record of Sovereign Almighty God fulfilling His eternal plans and purpose and the created angel Satan failing to stop Him.

God launched all of His Bible dreams in order to advance His own Kingdom plans and purpose. The key word is purpose, not purposes and that purpose is Jesus Christ. We see these same things happening in all of St Patrick's dreams.

The checklist I use is called,

The McCauley Dream Checklist

The Dream Setting/Backstory
The Dream Scripture
The Problem
The Dreamer's Metron
The Message
God's Purpose
Satan's Purpose
Dreamer's Eyes Enlightened

Dreamer's Response and Application
Know God Better
The Dream Process.
The Usual Suspects
Takeaways

ST PATRICK'S METRON

Understanding the biblical Greek term *metron* is really very helpful when it comes to making sense of dreams or any revelation.

The word metron refers to our God-given sphere of influence, our God-given responsibilities, concerning family, work, ministry, possessions, inheritance and so on.

All believers and non-believers have a specific metron for which they are responsible before God. Scripture says all authority comes from God and God will hold us responsible for how we exercise that authority.

A husband has responsibility for his wife and children. If he is a doctor his metron will also include his patients. If he is a cancer doctor his metron will include the cancer ward but will definitely not extend to the maternity unit.

A farmer's metron allows him to plant whatever seeds he wants in his own fields but gives him no permission to plant seeds in a neighbour's field. A pilot's metron covers only his own aeroplane.

When we understand our God-given sphere of influence, our metron, and stay within the orbit of our responsibilities we have little or no trouble. The problems start when we poke our noses into other people's metrons, other people's business.

Paul used the Greek term metron when explaining his God-given sphere of responsibility to the Church in Corinth. He said,

> We do not dare to classify or compare ourselves with some who commend themselves. When they measure themselves by themselves and compare themselves with themselves, they are not wise. We, however, will not boast beyond proper limits, (metron) but will confine our boasting to the sphere of service (metron) God himself has assigned to us, a sphere (metron) that also includes you.[1]

Paul is explaining God has given him influence and responsibility over the Corinthian Church. He has no metron or responsibility for the Jerusalem Church, which was under the metron of Peter, James and John.

Paul hoped the Corinthian church would grow and mature so his metron for spreading the Gospel amongst the gentiles would also expand. Paul was limited in his metron. Jesus on the other hand has an unlimited metron. He is the Alpha and the Omega. He has the Spirit without measure.

Like Paul we also have a limited metron relating to our present God-given responsibilities. The revelation we receive in dreams will always relate to our metron. Understanding this simple fact saves us untold trouble and helps us to stay focused and on track.

THE MCCAULEY DREAM CHECKLIST

THIS IS a checklist I created based on Paul's prayer for the Ephesians,

> I keep asking that the God of our Lord Jesus Christ, the glorious Father, may give you the Spirit of wisdom and revelation, so that you may know him better. I pray that the eyes of your heart may be enlightened in order that you may know the hope to which he has called you, the riches of his glorious inheritance in his holy people, and his incomparably great power for us who believe.[1]

For me the checklist provides a consistency and an

accountability to the interpretative process. It helps me stop cutting corners.

The McCauley Dream Checklist

The Dream Setting/Backstory
The Dream Scripture
The Problem
The Dreamer's Metron
The Message
God's Purpose
Satan's Purpose
Dreamer's Eyes Enlightened
Dreamer's Response and Application
Know God Better
The Dream Process.
The Usual Suspects
Takeaways

The Dream Setting/Backstory: Every dream typically arrives in the middle of a character's story and usually carries the answer to a problem. The Dream Setting/Backstory provides a context for the dream and allows us to get an idea of what's going on.

Understanding the context of the dream helps us get a better sense of what's occurring in the bigger picture.

Context refers to the surrounding background circumstances and the specific environment or situation the dreamer finds himself in. This enables us to grasp an overview of the situation and its meaning and how the dream fits in.

The Dream Scripture: The dream scripture is our main focus. It also usually includes a sense of context. It always contains the dream, the dreamer and their response. Sometimes the dream is immediately understood and applied. Other times it requires interpretation. Sometimes it's a simple message about a simple situation, other times it can be very complex with a whole world impact

The Problem: God's dreams tend to answer and deal with problems that threaten to derail His greater plans and purpose. Often the dreamer knows nothing about the problem. Usually it's a case of God taking the initiative and intervening in the dreamer's life and circumstances in order to both care for the dreamer and to advance God's Own Kingdom Agenda. Though in Patrick's case four dreams were sent in answer to prayer.

Yet often in Bible dreams God is regularly shown as *The Great Trouble Shooter*. Psalm 46 says,

> God is our refuge and strength,
> an ever-present help in trouble.
> Therefore we will not fear, though the
>   earth give way
> and the mountains fall into the heart of the
>   sea.[2]

The Dreamer's Metron: The dreamer's metron also adds context to the dream. Metron refers to the dreamer's level of authority and sphere of influence. God always sends His dream to a credible person who is in a position to either share the dream or implement the dream's instruction.

For example, Pharaoh's Cupbearer was totally unable to promote Joseph to a high position in Egypt but his metron allowed him to introduce Joseph to Pharaoh who did in fact have the metron to promote Joseph to the position God had intended for him.

The Message: The dream message is whatever communication God wants to give the dreamer in order to advance God's plans and purpose.

Many times it is clear and simple and can be taken literally. Other times it may be cryptic and symbolic and require an interpretation, occasionally by an angel.

It's also possible the dreamer will not understand the dream. Sometimes they just have to get on with their lives. After *Daniel's 'Ram, Goat and Little Horn' Dream* the prophet said,

> I, Daniel, was worn out. I lay exhausted for several days. Then I got up and went about the king's business. I was appalled by the vision; it was beyond understanding.[3]

Other times the dream message can be implemented immediately like Joseph instantly taking Mary and Jesus to a place of safety. With other dreams it can take years like Joseph with Pharaoh and sometimes like Daniel's dream it has to be sealed up for the distant future.[4]

God's Purpose: God who sustains all things by his powerful word, including billions of people, billions of planets and billions of galaxies, does nothing without purpose.[5]

Paul said God's mysterious purpose is that through the gospel the Gentiles are fellow heirs, fellow members of the body, and fellow partakers of the promise in Christ Jesus.[6]

He also spoke of God's ongoing purpose which is,

> Through the church, the manifold wisdom of God should be made known to the rulers and authorities in the heavenly

realms, according to the eternal purpose that He accomplished in Christ Jesus our Lord.[7]

God's four main purposes for Bible dreams were,

1. To demonstrate His dominion over all the powers and principalities.
2. To encourage and guide His Covenant People with specific directions for their well-being and the safety of their seed line.
3. To prevent people and kings from harming His Covenant People and their seed line and to provide for His Covenant People and their seed line.
4. To encourage and help His New Testament Covenant People carry out the Great Commission of Jesus Christ.

Satan's Purpose: Jesus said, Satan comes only to steal and kill and destroy[8]. He also told Peter, Satan has asked to sift all of you as wheat[9] and Peter told us all to,

> Be alert and of sober mind. Your enemy the devil prowls around like a roaring lion looking for someone to devour.[10]

Satan's main mission is to thwart God's plans and

purpose for humanity's redemption. As regards God's dreams Satan's primary focus was to destroy the Royal seed line of the woman so the Messiah could not come forth.

Today he still works to kill as many people as possible before they can come to the saving knowledge of Jesus Christ and take their rightful place in God's kingdom.

The proper interpretation and application of a dream from God always harms Satan's kingdom.

Dreamer's Eyes Enlightened: This focuses us to examine just how much the dreamer comprehends God's message and to what extent they understand what God requires of them.

Dreamer's Response and Application: This allows us to see the dreamer's heart concerning their conformity to God's will and their obedience in doing God's will. The vast majority of dreamers are immediately obedient to God's will. One notable exception was Solomon whose longterm disobedience was tragic for Israel.

Know God Better: This section enables us to see God in action and to understand what's really important to Him. We also get to see His various attributes in action as He deals with His beloved Covenant people, the powers and principalities, humanity and His Only Beloved Son.

We were all born to know God. The purpose of all revelation is to know Him better.[11] Dreams are a main way God reveals His plans and purpose. Yet after a zillion years, when Satan has been defeated and the kingdom of this world has become the kingdom of our Lord and of his Messiah,[12] our primary goal will still be to know Him better.

The Dream Process: In the dream process we consider the nuts and bolts of the dream in order to seek for meaning and an interpretation. We ask who, what, where and when questions like, Who is it for? What does it concern? When will it happen? What weight does it carry? Is it of individual or national importance or does it have a spiritual impact through eons of time?

Is it literal or symbolic? Does it require interpretation? Does is contain, God, Jesus, Holy Spirit, angels etc. Does it contain a warning, an encouragement, directions or rebuke?

Usually we also consider the significance of various objects within the dream. For example in *Nebuchadnezzar's Large Statue Dream* we might try to figure out the importance and meaning of the head made of pure gold, the chest and arms of silver, the belly and thighs of bronze, the legs of iron and the feet partly of iron and partly of baked clay.

We'd certainly want to know what the rock not cut by human hands symbolised.

The Usual Suspects: This is a category I included for my own entertainment. God, Jesus, and Holy Spirit are all over the Bible often hidden in plain sight. Many of us are like the two disciples on the road to Emmaus.[13] We often can't join the dots up.

Satan is also all over the place trying to hinder God's plans. In this section I peek for evidence of God, Jesus, Holy Spirit and Satan in the dream.

Takeaways: Takaways are lessons, applications, key points revelations and so on, worth noting and remembering as regards the dream.

ST PATRICK'S FIRST DREAM
'YOU HAVE FASTED WELL'

The Dream Setting/Backstory

Patrick was kidnapped from Bannavem Taburniae, an unknown place outside of Ireland. Although he was the son of Calpornius a deacon and the grandson of Potitus a priest, Patrick had no personal relationship with God.

At age sixteen he was taken as a slave to Ireland. Patrick said he deserved this punishment because of his careless attitude and neglect of God. But God was merciful. He convicted Patrick for his lack of faith, and protected him as a loving father. Patrick's response was to turn wholeheartedly to God. He writes,

After I arrived in Ireland, I tended sheep every day, and I prayed frequently during the day. More and more the love of God increased, and my sense of awe before God. Faith grew, and my spirit was moved, so that in one day I would pray up to one hundred times, and at night perhaps the same. I even remained in the woods and on the mountain, and I would rise to pray before dawn in snow and ice and rain. I never felt the worse for it, and I never felt lazy – as I realise now, the Spirit was burning in me at that time.[1]

The Dream Scripture

It was there one night in my sleep that I heard a voice saying to me: "You have fasted well. Very soon you will return to your native country."

The Problem

Patrick spent six years tending sheep and pigs in harsh conditions yet in God's purpose these years were critical to his spiritual development. God used this time to reveal

Himself to Patrick and to fill Patrick with His Holy Spirit so that at age twenty two Patrick was an intercessor filled with the Holy Spirit and fire. Once again God needed to change Patrick's circumstances in order to move His plans and purpose forward. So He sent a dream.

The Dreamer's Metron

Saint Patrick was a fifth-century Romano-British Christian missionary and bishop credited with bringing Christianity to parts of Ireland. He baptised thousands of people and ordained many priests to lead the new Christian communities. He converted wealthy women, some of whom became nuns in the face of family opposition.

He also dealt with the sons of kings, converting them too. He also preached to his slavers. Patrick was baptised in the Holy Spirit and fire and spoke in tongues and prophesied. He was also a big dreamer of dreams. Approximately one quarter of Patrick's book, *The Confession* concerns dreams from God that he received and obeyed.

Patrick was also partly responsible for the Christianisation of the Picts and Anglo-Saxons. Although never formally canonised, Patrick became known as the Apostle of Ireland and is venerated as a saint in the Catholic Church, the Lutheran Church, the Church of Ireland and in the Eastern Orthodox Church where he is regarded as equal-to-the-apostles and Enlightener of Ireland.

Patrick was also a scribe, the first person to write an autobiographical piece in the early Irish church. He strongly opposed slavery and sex trafficking as seen in his, *Letter To The Soldiers of Coroticus*. He also wrote *The Confession*, to counteract accusations made against him. It's possible the *Letter To The Soldiers of Coroticus* provoked a clerical and political backlash that resulted in the trial which Patrick mentions in *The Confession*.

During his lifetime Patrick's metron was confined to Ireland but in these last days, God has increased Patrick's influence all over the world. Perhaps that's why Satan has come up with green beer, hangovers, and dancing leprechauns.

The Message

God affirmed Patrick's fast has been accepted. God also told Patrick he'd soon return to his home in Bannavem Taburniae.

God's Purpose

God's purpose was to encourage and produce faith in Patrick so he'd have the courage to flee slavery and undertake a 200 mile journey as a solitary fugitive in an unfamiliar and dangerous land.

Satan's Purpose

Satan's purpose was to have Patrick remain a slave in a pagan nation.

Dreamer's Eyes Enlightened

Patrick understood God had accepted his praying and fasting, and was happy with him. He also realised God was going to release him from slavery and return him home to his family.

Dreamer's Response and Application

Patrick believed God's voice and this produced faith for further revelation and for the actual event to take place.

Know God Better

Sovereign God was able to encourage and affirm His servant. He was also able to give a prophetic word through a dream that released Patrick into a future where he could bless God's children in Ireland. God had already accomplished something similar through His servant Joseph in the Book Of Genesis.

The Dream Process

This was a simple literal guidance dream in which Patrick heard a voice. In Patrick's first two dreams we're not specifically told about the source of the voice. I think we can safely assume it was God's voice for it is always God's voice in Patrick's other dreams apart from the voice of the Irish Dream. This dream needs no interpretation, only the faith to believe.

The Usual Suspects

God's spoke to Patrick through His Holy Spirit and the purpose was to equip Patrick further to be able to bring the gospel of Jesus Christ to the Irish nation. Satan was evident in the slavery.

Takeaways

Isaiah 58 speaks about the type of fasting that pleases God. God is not pleased with people who outwardly religiously fast but continue to please themselves, exploit their workers and fight and cause strife. Rather, God says.

> "Is this not the fast that I have chosen:
> To loose the bonds of wickedness,
> To undo the heavy burdens,

> To let the oppressed go free,
> And that you break every yoke?
> Is it not to share your bread with the hungry,
> And that you bring to your house the poor who are cast out;
> When you see the naked, that you cover him.[2]

These are the very things Patrick practised during his ministry in Ireland as he announced the year of the Lord's favour to the nation,

> The Spirit of the Sovereign Lord is on me,
> because the Lord has anointed me
> to proclaim good news to the poor.
> He has sent me to bind up the broken-hearted,
> to proclaim freedom for the captives
> and release from darkness for the prisoners,
> to proclaim the year of the Lord's favor
> and the day of vengeance of our God,
> to comfort all who mourn,
> and provide for those who grieve in Zion—
> to bestow on them a crown of beauty instead of ashes, the oil of joy

   instead of mourning and a garment of
     praise
   instead of a spirit of despair. They will
     be called oaks of righteousness, a plant-
     ing of the Lord   for the display of his
     splendour.[3]

ST PATRICK'S SECOND DREAM
'YOUR SHIP IS READY'

The Dream Setting/Backstory

PATRICK HAD BEEN a slave in Ireland for six years. It was now time to move things forward in God's plans and purpose. So God spoke to him in a dream. Patrick wrote, I heard a voice saying to me: "You have fasted well. Very soon you will return to your native country." Then God sent this second dream.

The Dream Scripture

Again after a short while, I heard someone saying to me: "Look – your ship is ready." It was not nearby, but a good two hundred miles away. I had never been to the place, nor did I know anyone there. So I ran away then, and left the man with whom I had been for six years. It was in the strength of God that I went – God who turned the direction of my life to good; I feared nothing while I was on the journey to that ship.

The Problem

Patrick spent six years tending sheep and pigs in very harsh conditions. These years were critical to his spiritual development. God used them to reveal Himself to Patrick and to fill Patrick with His promised Holy Spirit. Aged twenty two, Patrick was now an intercessor filled with the Holy Spirit and fire. God once again needed to change Patrick's circumstances in order to move His plans and purpose for Patrick forward. So He sent a dream.

The Dreamer's Metron

Saint Patrick was a fifth-century Romano-British Christian missionary and bishop credited with bringing Christianity to parts of Ireland. He baptised thousands of people and ordained many priests to lead the new Christian communities. He converted wealthy women, some of whom became nuns in the face of family opposition.

He also dealt with the sons of kings, converting them too. He also preached to his slavers. Patrick was baptised in the Holy Spirit and fire and spoke in tongues and prophesied. He was also a big dreamer of dreams. Approximately one quarter of Patrick's book, *The*

Confession concerns dreams from God that he received and obeyed.

Patrick was also partly responsible for the Christianisation of the Picts and Anglo-Saxons. Although never formally canonised, Patrick became known as the Apostle of Ireland and is venerated as a saint in the Catholic Church, the Lutheran Church, the Church of Ireland and in the Eastern Orthodox Church where he is regarded as equal-to-the-apostles and Enlightener of Ireland.

Patrick was also a scribe, the first person to write an autobiographical piece in the early Irish church. He strongly opposed slavery and sex trafficking as seen in his, *Letter To The Soldiers of Coroticus*.

He also wrote *The Confession*, to counteract accusations made against him. It's possible the *Letter To The Soldiers of Coroticus* provoked a clerical and political backlash that resulted in the trial which Patrick mentions in *The Confession*.

During his lifetime Patrick's metron was confined to Ireland but in these last days, for some reason, God has increased Patrick's influence all over the world. Perhaps that's why Satan has come up with green beer, hangovers and dancing leprechauns.

The Message

God told Patrick his ship of escape was now ready.

God also showed Patrick the location of the ship 200 miles away.

God's Purpose

God was relocating Patrick for the next stage of His plans and purpose. God's purpose was to produce faith in Patrick through this dream. Romans 10:17 says, So then faith comes by hearing, and hearing by the word of God. A dream from God is a word from God. It produces faith. See Takeaway section below.

Satan's Purpose

Satan's purpose was to have Patrick live and die as a lonely slave in a pagan nation. He didn't want Patrick to hear and believe God in his dreams. He wanted Patrick to be afraid and remain a slave for the rest of his life.

Dreamer's Eyes Enlightened

Patrick knew the timing was right to make good his escape. He was also shown where the ship was waiting in a port 200 miles away.

Dreamer's Response and Application

Patrick immediately obeyed God's instructions and headed off towards the waiting ship. His obedience released God's strength and courage into his life. Patrick had no fear whatsoever on this dangerous journey.

Know God Better

God's dreams are always sent for a reason. All of God's dreams to Patrick were totally focused on God caring for Patrick and guiding him to where he should live at any particular time. World history was now at the stage where Jesus had defeated Satan and the other gods through the work of The Cross. It was now God's time for the nations to receive the blessing promised to Abraham.[1] God was also keeping his promise to Adam and Eve of crushing Satan's head[2] by sending Patrick to Ireland.

The Dream Process

This was a literal guidance dream in which Patrick heard a voice. In Patrick's first two dreams we're not specifically told about the source of the voice. I think we can safely assume it is God's voice. It's always God's voice in the other dreams apart from the Voice of the Irish Dream.

This dream also needs no interpretation. Only the faith to believe. It seems God showed Patrick the ship and its location 200 miles away. We're not told how this part happened. Perhaps it was a visionary experience because the voice said, Look!

Unfortunately we don't know anymore than that.

The Usual Suspects

Similar to the first first dream, God spoke to Patrick through His Holy Spirit and the purpose was to equip Patrick to be able to bring the gospel of Jesus Christ to the Irish nation. Satan was evident in the slavery and in the dangerous 200 mile journey.

Takeaways

Patrick's situation was similar to Joseph's circumstances in the Old Testament. God was constantly in charge of Joseph's life circumstances and was working out His sovereign purpose through Joseph in the midst of great hostility and bitterness.

When things were at their worst, God was still in control. Even though Joseph would suffer thirteen years of exile and hardship there was nothing Satan or man could do to stop God's plans and purpose coming to pass. Psalm 105 says,

> He sent a man before them, even Joseph, who was sold for a servant: Whose feet they hurt with fetters: he was laid in irons: Until the time that his word came to pass, the word of the Lord tested him.

In this verse the dreams from God to Joseph are called the word of the Lord. It was the dreams, as the word of God, that tested Joseph. Joseph passed the test by believing in God's dreams to him and God's promises despite adverse outward circumstances.

The word of God is vitally important to a believer. Jesus told Satan, Man shall not live on bread alone, but on every word that comes from the mouth of God.[3] Paul similarly said, So then faith comes by hearing, and hearing by the word of God.[4]

A dream from God is a word from God. It can sustain us, like Joseph, through many years. A dream as the word of God also produces faith and faith leads to action. We see this at work in all of Patrick's dreams.

God often conveys His plans and purposes to us through dreams as His word. When we receive and understand these messages of God's word we receive faith to be God's representatives in bringing to pass His specific communicated plans and purpose.

Patrick's *Your Ship Is Ready* Dream similarly produces enough faith in Patrick that he is willing to risk his life by deserting his slave master and embarking on a 200 mile perilous journey.

In fact, this dream as the word of God produced so much faith that Patrick was able to say,

> It was in the strength of God that I went – God who turned the direction of my life to good; I feared nothing while I was on the journey to that ship.[5]

ST PATRICK'S THIRD DREAM
'SATAN TESTED PATRICK'

The Dream Setting/Backstory

GOD SENT this dream a couple of months after the previous one. Patrick had managed to board his ship of escape only after an answer to prayer. When the seamen were starving Patrick preached to them. He also prayed and received a miraculous provision of food. This resulted in the sailors praising God and honouring Patrick. Patrick's spiritual success resulted in a direct physical attack from Satan when he was asleep.

The Dream Scripture

That same night while I was sleeping, Satan strongly put me to the test – I will remember it as long as I live! It was as if an enormous rock fell on me, and I lost all power in my limbs. Although I knew little about the life of the spirit at the time, how was it that I knew to call upon Helias? While these things were happening, I saw the sun rise in the sky, and while I was calling "Helias! Helias!" with all my strength, the splendour of the sun fell on me; and immediately, all that weight was lifted from me. I believe that I was helped by Christ the Lord, and that his spirit cried out for me. I trust that it will be like this whenever I am under stress, as the gospel says: "In that day, the Lord testifies, it will not be you who will speak, but the Spirit of your Father who speaks in you."

The Problem

Patrick's success in overcoming Satan's hindering strategies to prevent him returning home, resulted in a direct personal attack from Satan.

The Dreamer's Metron

Saint Patrick was a fifth-century Romano-British Christian missionary and bishop credited with bringing Christianity to parts of Ireland. He baptised thousands of people and ordained many priests to lead the new Christian communities. He converted wealthy women, some of whom became nuns in the face of family opposition.

He also dealt with the sons of kings, converting them too. He also preached to his slavers. Patrick was baptised in the Holy Spirit and fire and spoke in tongues and prophesied. He was also a big dreamer of dreams. Approximately one quarter of Patrick's book, *The Confession* concerns dreams from God that he received and obeyed.

Patrick was also partly responsible for the Christianisation of the Picts and Anglo-Saxons. Although never formally canonised, Patrick became known as the Apostle of Ireland and is venerated as a saint in the Catholic Church, the Lutheran Church, the Church of Ireland and in the Eastern Orthodox Church where he is regarded as equal-to-the-apostles and Enlightener of Ireland.

Patrick was also a scribe, the first person to write an autobiographical piece in the early Irish church. He strongly opposed slavery and sex trafficking as seen in his, *Letter To The Soldiers of Coroticus*. He also wrote *The Confession*, to counteract accusations made against him.

It's possible the *Letter To The Soldiers of Coroticus* provoked a clerical and political backlash that resulted in the trial which Patrick mentions in *The Confession*.

During his lifetime Patrick's metron was confined to Ireland but in these last days, for some reason, God has increased Patrick's influence all over the world. Perhaps that's why Satan has come up with green beer, hangovers and dancing leprechauns.

The Message

The basic message from this symbolic dream is that God will never leave or forsake Patrick.[1] Psalm 50:15 says, Call upon Me in the day of trouble; I will deliver you, and you shall glorify Me." Psalm 34:17 similarly says, The Lord hears his people when they call to him for help. He rescues them from all their troubles.

God's Purpose

God's purpose was to bring Patrick back to Bannavem Taburniae so Patrick could become a priest and be better equipped to be a missionary to Ireland. God was well able to deliver Patrick from all hindering attacks of Satan and fulfil His plans and purpose for Patrick's life. He also wanted to give Patrick an experience of speaking in tongues and an insight into how this gift actually operates.

Satan's Purpose

Satan's purpose as usual was to steal, and to kill, and to destroy.[2] This was a direct attack on Patrick's life and future. Satan fell like a rock upon Patrick and drained him of all power. No doubt he would have killed him if possible. Satan was inflamed at Patrick's success.

The Scripture says, The reason the Son of God appeared was to destroy the devil's work.[3] The book of Acts also says,

> God anointed Jesus of Nazareth with the Holy Ghost and with power, and He went about doing good and healing all who were oppressed by the devil, for God was with Him.[4]

Satan had seen Jesus and His disciples destroy his works in Israel, Europe, Asia and other nations. Now Jesus was doing the same thing in Ireland. Patrick, although not yet a priest, was well able to preach and proclaim the word of God to the starving sailors and see God move on their behalf. Patrick told them.

> Turn in faith with all your hearts to the Lord my God, because nothing is impossible for him so that he may put food in your way – even enough to make you fully satisfied! He has an abundance everywhere.[5]

Dreamer's Eyes Enlightened

Patrick knew he was no match for Satan in his own strength. He realised it was a case of, 'Not by might nor by power, but by my Spirit,' says the Lord Almighty.[6]

This was a very important lesson for Patrick's life's mission. He also understood it was God's work and not Patrick's work. God's strength not Patrick's strength. Jesus similarly encouraged His disciples when he said,

> You will stand trial before governors and kings because you are my followers. But this will be your opportunity to tell the rulers and other unbelievers about me. When you are arrested, don't worry about how to respond or what to say. God will give you the right words at the right time. For it is not you who will be speaking—it will be the Spirit of your Father speaking through you.[7]

Patrick knew it was Jesus who gave him the word Helias. This was the word that caused the deliverance. He also knew it was the Holy Spirit who was speaking through him.

Dreamer's Response and Application

Patrick understood it was Christ's Spirit who caused him to call out, 'Helias! Helias!' Patrick did this with all his spiritual strength because Satan had robbed him of all physical power. Patrick's response to the overall experience was to interpret and understand it as an application of Matthew 10:20, which says, 'It will not be you who will speak, but the Spirit of your Father who speaks in you.'[8] So, in fact it was the Holy Spirit speaking in Patrick that caused him to proclaim Helias. See Takaways below.

Know God Better

God uses this satanic test to teach Patrick a few things. Firstly, Patrick was no match for Satan in his own strength. Secondly God was always with Patrick to deliver him from all his enemies. Thirdly, the work Patrick would do in Ireland would be the work of the Holy Spirit done in the power of the Holy Spirit.

Patrick didn't need to know the future. The Holy Spirit Who indwelled him was well able for anything Patrick might encounter in his ministry. This removed all fear from Patrick.

Fourthly God used the situation as an opportunity to show Patrick that His word is dependable and true. God also gave Patrick a dream like experience that showed speaking in tongues can defeat the work of the devil.

The Dream Process

This is a symbolic protection dream that provides interesting information yet leaves us with some unanswered questions. We know Satan fell upon Patrick when he was sleeping and drained him of all physical strength. We don't know if Patrick woke up at this stage or if he remained sleeping and the rest of the action happened within a dream.

We know Patrick was surprised when he began calling out the word, Helias. He wondered, How was it that I knew to call upon Helias? We also know Patrick was calling upon someone for help, but we don't know who. We're never told what Helias means.

We do know Patrick was delivered from the Satanic attack when he kept declaring the name Helias. We don't know if Patrick was asleep in a dream at this point or if he had wakened up to a physical sun.

We do know Patrick was helped by Christ the Lord, and that God's Spirit cried out for him. This means Jesus likely gave Patrick the word Helias. It also means the Holy Spirit was speaking the word Helias through Patrick. This is why Patrick makes the remark about life in the spirit.

It's also why he quotes the scripture that says, In that day, the Lord testifies, it will not be you who will speak, but the Spirit of your Father who speaks in you. Patrick knew the Holy Spirit was using his voice to speak a word of deliverance given by Jesus.

In this dream experience Patrick was functioning in the spiritual gift of speaking in tongues and it was this gift in operation that destroyed Satan's attack.

The Holy Spirit enabled Patrick to speak 'Helias' and afterwards Patrick gave an interpretation that said,

> I believe that I was helped by Christ the Lord, and that his spirit cried out for me. I trust that it will be like this whenever I am under stress, as the gospel says: "In that day, the Lord testifies, it will not be you who will speak, but the Spirit of your Father who speaks in you."

The Usual Suspects

Satan is present like a rock crushing the life out of Patrick. God the Father, Jesus, and the Holy Spirit are clearly in the midst of the action and in the scripture the Holy Spirit brought to Patrick's mind. Jesus said concerning the Holy Spirit,

> But the Helper, the Holy Spirit, whom the Father will send in My name, He will teach you all things, and bring to your remembrance all things that I said to you.[9]

Takeaways

The use of the word 'Helias' in this dream requires

comment. Some critics have suggested 'Helias' might refer to Helios the sun god. After all the Irish were sun worshippers. But this notion makes no sense because the sun god Helios could not have delivered Patrick from Satan. Jesus taught that devils don't cast out devils. He said,

> And if Satan cast out Satan, he is divided against himself; how shall then his kingdom stand?[10]

The ancient Irish hagiographic spin-doctor, Muirchú, suggested the word 'Helias' might better be translated into Elijah, as if Patrick was calling out for help from Elijah in his battle with Satan.

Interestingly, when Jesus was dying in the afternoon darkness, He called out in a loud voice, *"Eli, Eli, lema sabachthani?"* (which means "My God, my God, why have you forsaken me?")[11]

Some of the bystanders heard this, and wrongly said, "He's calling Elijah."

One modern scribe, claims Patrick's actual words have been lost as one copyist altered them in allusion to the Kyrie eleison of his contemporary liturgy and another copyist failed to detect the allusion, and so corrected the eleison in reference to Elijah instead.

This writer says, the context suggests Patrick's original words would have been a simple cry for mercy addressed to Christ, just like the eleison itself. The prayer, Kyrie, eleison means, Lord, have mercy.

This interpretation seems to make some sense for if Satan suddenly fell upon you like a great rock and all your power left you, it's quite possible you might cry out, Lord have mercy.

That's what most believers would do. But Patrick says something that goes beyond this point. He wrote, Although I knew little about the life of the spirit at the time, how was it that I knew to call upon Helias?

What Patrick is saying here is that his calling upon 'Helias' was an issue concerned with the life of the Holy Spirit. So, Patrick's cry of 'Helias' was obviously different from a normal everyday cry for help from God.

Patrick was surprised he was calling "Helias! Helias!" with all his strength. This wasn't natural for him. He said, Although I knew little about the life of the spirit at the time, how was it that I knew to call upon Helias? Patrick knew his strong cries of Helias came from the Holy Spirit and not from his own mind.

Patrick also believed he was helped in making his cries of Helias by Christ the Lord, and that Christ's Spirit cried out for him. To this end, Patrick quotes the scripture that says, it will not be you who will speak, but the Spirit of your Father who speaks in you.[12]

The obvious interpretation of this incident is that Patrick was speaking in tongues because the word Helias was not coming from his own mind. He was being helped by the Holy Spirit. This is how speaking in tongues occurs. That's the way I speak in tongues and it's the way I've heard thousands of other believers speak in tongues over the years.

This agrees with Paul's teaching in 1 Corinthians 14:14 which says, For if I pray in a tongue, my spirit prays, but my mind is unfruitful. The New Living Version says it simpler, For if I pray in tongues, my spirit is praying, but I don't understand what I am saying.

Patrick didn't understand what he was saying but he knew it was the Holy Spirit that was speaking and he knew it was the Holy Spirit who brought him a release from Satan's attack.

Perhaps the translator from the Latin didn't know what the word Helias meant either and perhaps no one has ever properly interpreted it because Helias might even be the tongue of an angel.[13]

Another Possible Interpretation

There may be another level of interpretation if in fact 'Helias' refers to the sun. In that case, 'Helias' in context could reference Jesus as the Sun of God and also symbolically refer to the actual sun. Remember this is a symbolic dream experience and literal and symbolic themes often coexist in dreams.

Patrick was powerless under the weight of Satan in the darkness. He then called upon Helias which might represent Jesus as the heavenly Sun and also refer to the literal sun for when the splendour of the literal sun fell upon Patrick, Satan's attack was immediately destroyed by Jesus, and the darkness was gone.

When this happened Patrick immediately said, I believe that I was helped by Christ the Lord, and that His spirit cried out for me.

Patrick didn't say he was helped by the sun god Helios or by Elijah. Nowhere else in his writings does Patrick ever invoke the name of Elijah or any other saint.

Patrick clearly knew he was helped by Christ and realised it was the Holy Spirit that caused him to keep exclaiming 'Helias'.

And, all of this happened even though Patrick knew little about the life of the spirit at the time.

In this *'Satan Tested Patrick' Dream* we again see Patrick being helped by Christ's Holy Spirit just as he was in the *Jesus Speaks Within You Dream* and *The Spirit Helps Our Weakness Dream*.

The mature Patrick when writing his biography interprets the experience by a scripture from Jesus. He writes,

> I trust that it will be like this whenever I am under stress, as the gospel says: "In that day, the Lord testifies, it will not be you who will speak, but the Spirit of your Father who speaks in you."[14]

There is another scripture that might throw some light on this dream. Patrick used it later in *The Confession*. That scripture concerns the final words of Malachi the Old Testament,

> Surely the day is coming; it will burn like a furnace. All the arrogant and every evildoer will be stubble, and the day that is coming will set them on fire, says the Lord Almighty. Not a root or a branch will be left to them.
> But for you who revere my name, the sun of righteousness will rise with healing in its rays. And you will go out and frolic like well-fed calves. Then you will trample on the wicked; they will be ashes under the soles of your feet on the day when I act, says the Lord Almighty.
> Remember the law of my servant Moses, the decrees and laws I gave him at Horeb for all Israel.
> See, I will send the prophet Elijah to you before that great and dreadful day of the Lord comes. He will turn the hearts of the parents to their children, and the hearts of the children to their parents; or else I will come and strike the land with total destruction.[15]

Here we see it is Jesus who is being called the sun of righteousness. Other versions make it more explicit by translating it as the Sun of Righteousness. It is Jesus who rises with healing in His wings and it is Jesus who sets the captives free.

We also have a reference to Elijah turning the hearts of the fathers to the children. Perhaps this is what influenced Muirchú, to suggest 'Helias' might be translated into Elijah.

Later in his normal daily mission Patrick would have been constantly telling the Irish that it wasn't the sun in the sky they should worship but the Son who made the sun in the sky - The Sun Of Righteousness.[16]

Later in his writing, Patrick plainly articulates his position on the natural sun and the heavenly Sun. He wrote,

> The sun which we see rising for us each day at his command, that sun will never reign, nor will its splendour continue forever; and all those who adore that sun will come to a bad, miserable penalty.
> We, however, believe in and adore the true sun, that is, Christ, who will never perish. Nor will they perish who do his will but they will abide forever just as Christ will abide forever.
> He lives with God the Father almighty and

with the Holy Spirit before the ages began, and now, and for all the ages of ages. Amen.[17]

Even though there is no way to know with certainty what Helias means we are 100% sure it was Jesus who rescued Patrick from Satan. We are also 100% sure Jesus provided the word Helias and 100% sure the Holy Spirit caused Patrick to keep speaking this word until he was delivered from Satan.

ST PATRICK'S FOURTH DREAM
'TWO MONTHS IN CAPTIVITY'

The Dream Setting/Backstory

ST PATRICK WASN'T chronological in his writings. We just know this dream came a number of years after the *Satan Tested Patrick Dream*.

The Dream Scripture

> It happened again after many years that I was taken a prisoner. On the first night I was with them, I heard a divine answer saying to me: "You will be with them for two months." This is how it was: on the sixtieth night, the Lord freed me from their hands.

The Problem

Patrick has been captured again and was praying about how long he'd be a prisoner.

The Dreamer's Metron

Saint Patrick was a fifth-century Romano-British Christian missionary and bishop credited with bringing Christianity to parts of Ireland. He baptised thousands of people and ordained many priests to lead the new Christian communities. He converted wealthy women, some of whom became nuns in the face of family opposition.

He also dealt with the sons of kings, converting them too. He also preached to his slavers. Patrick was baptised in the Holy Spirit and fire and spoke in tongues and prophesied. He was also a big dreamer of dreams. Approximately one quarter of Patrick's book, *The Confession* concerns dreams from God that he received and obeyed.

Patrick was also partly responsible for the Christianisation of the Picts and Anglo-Saxons. Although never formally canonised, Patrick became known as the Apostle of Ireland and is venerated as a saint in the Catholic Church, the Lutheran Church, the Church of Ireland and in the Eastern Orthodox Church where he is regarded as equal-to-the-apostles and Enlightener of Ireland.

Patrick was also a scribe, the first person to write an autobiographical piece in the early Irish church. He strongly opposed slavery and sex trafficking as seen in his, *Letter To The Soldiers of Coroticus*. He also wrote *The Confession*, to counteract accusations made against him.

It's possible the *Letter To The Soldiers of Coroticus* provoked a clerical and political backlash that resulted in the trial which Patrick mentions in *The Confession*.

During his lifetime Patrick's metron was confined to Ireland but in these last days, for some reason, God has increased Patrick's influence all over the world. Perhaps that's why Satan has come up with green beer, hangovers and dancing leprechauns.

The Message

God told Patrick he'd be held captive for two months.

God's Purpose

God's sovereign purpose was to answer Patrick's prayer and let him know exactly what was happening. God showed Patrick He was in control of Patrick's life and situation.

Satan's Purpose

Satan's purpose was to hinder God's purpose for Patrick's life. He wanted to enslave or kill Patrick.

Dreamer's Eyes Enlightened

Patrick immediately knew the time frame of his captivity.

Dreamer's Response and Application

Patrick believed God's instruction and waited patiently for his release.

Know God Better

All Biblical prophecy came from a sovereign God who communicated directly through His prophets to His people. God's revelation came directly from God.

In the same way God's dreams communicate God's thoughts and not man's thoughts. No recorded Bible dream ever originated from the mind of the dreamer.

This is where the water has been muddied. Bible dreams did not come from man's consciousness, man's unconsciousness or Carl Jung's idea of the collective unconsciousness.

All Biblical dreams came from a sovereign God who

intervened into human history in order to further His own plans and purpose. All recorded Bible dreams came supernaturally from outside the dreamer. That's what's happening here. God is communicating with His servant Patrick, putting his mind at peace and showing His sovereignty.

The Dream Process

This is a literal guidance dream in which a divine voice says, You will be with them for two months. It was a clear personal message for Patrick who knew it was an answer to prayer. He calls it a divine answer.

The Usual Suspects

Satan is seen in Patrick's captivity. God is seen in the sovereign, specific answer to prayer and Patrick is released to spread the gospel of Jesus Christ in the power of the Holy Spirit.

Takeaways

All of God's dreams have a personal impact on the dreamer. In this dream Patrick was assured of God's ongoing protection.

Although God's dreams always advance God's greater plans and purpose they all contain some personal element relating to the dreamer's metron and life situation.

The dreamer always has skin in the game, something to gain and something to lose.

That's why God's dreams tend to have national, international and eternal significance. God is always moving His purpose for Jesus Christ forward.

ST PATRICK'S FIFTH DREAM
'THE CALL OF THE IRISH'

The Dream Setting/Backstory

PATRICK WROTE, A few years later I was again with my parents in Britain. They welcomed me as a son, and they pleaded with me that, after all the many tribulations I had undergone, I should never leave them again.[1]

The Dream Scripture

> It was while I was there that I saw, in a vision in the night, a man whose name was Victoricus coming as it were from Ireland with so many letters they could not be counted. He gave me one of these, and I read the beginning of the letter, the voice of the Irish people.

> While I was reading out the beginning of the letter, I thought I heard at that moment the voice of those who were beside the wood of Voclut, near the western sea. They called out as it were with one voice: "We beg you, holy boy, to come and walk again among us."
> This touched my heart deeply, and I could not read any further; I woke up then. Thanks be to God, after many years the Lord granted them what they were calling for.[2]

The Problem

Patrick's parents wanted him to remain at home while it was God's plan for him to return to Ireland as a missionary.

The Dreamer's Metron

Saint Patrick was a fifth-century Romano-British Christian missionary and bishop credited with bringing Christianity to parts of Ireland. He baptised thousands of people and ordained many priests to lead the new Christian communities. He converted wealthy women, some of whom became nuns in the face of family opposition.

He also dealt with the sons of kings, converting them

too. He also preached to his slavers. Patrick was baptised in the Holy Spirit and fire and spoke in tongues and prophesied. He was also a big dreamer of dreams. Approximately one quarter of Patrick's book, *The Confession* concerns dreams from God that he received and obeyed.

Patrick was also partly responsible for the Christianisation of the Picts and Anglo-Saxons. Although never formally canonised, Patrick became known as the Apostle of Ireland and is venerated as a saint in the Catholic Church, the Lutheran Church, the Church of Ireland and in the Eastern Orthodox Church where he is regarded as equal-to-the-apostles and Enlightener of Ireland.

Patrick was also a scribe, the first person to write an autobiographical piece in the early Irish church. He strongly opposed slavery and sex trafficking as seen in his, *Letter To The Soldiers of Coroticus.* He also wrote *The Confession*, to counteract accusations made against him.

It's possible the *Letter To The Soldiers of Coroticus* provoked a clerical and political backlash that resulted in the trial which Patrick mentions in *The Confession.*

During his lifetime Patrick's metron was confined to Ireland but in these last days, for some reason, God has increased Patrick's influence all over the world. Perhaps that's why Satan has come up with green beer, hangovers and dancing leprechauns.

The Message

The prayer message from the people of Ireland to Patrick was, We beg you, holy boy, to come and walk again among us.

God's Purpose

God's purpose was to touch Patrick's heart with a love for the poor pagan Irish so he'd return to Ireland with the Gospel.

Satan's Purpose

Satan's purpose was to have Patrick remain safely at home with his parents and stay away from God's calling for his life.

Dreamer's Eyes Enlightened

Patrick could both see and hear the call of the Irish. He knew they wanted and needed him.

Dreamer's Response and Application

Patrick's heart was deeply touched by this dream. He responded by being obedient to the call of the Irish and the call of God. In later years he gave thanks to God for answering the pleas and prayers of the Irish.

Know God Better

Sovereign God who created Patrick in his mother's womb knew exactly what would move Patrick's heart and motivate him to follow God's plan for his life.

The Dream Process

This is a symbolic calling dream with guidance. It involved sight and sound and required interpretation. A mysterious Christian called *Victoricus* appears, as if from Ireland, with a multitude of letters one of which has written on it, *The Voice of the Irish.*

Then, as Patrick begins to read one letter he actually hears the voice of Irish people he lived amongst calling him to come and walk amongst them once again. Patrick was so touched by their pleading he couldn't read any further.

The letters symbolised the prayers of the Irish for help and salvation. Patrick interprets all this as God's call for him to return to Ireland as a missionary. This calling dream impacts Ireland and many other nations.

The Usual Suspects

God sent this dream to show Patrick that the prayers of the Irish, who were enslaved by Satan, could only be answered by the gospel of Jesus Christ being preached in the power of the Holy Spirit

Takeaways

Some hagiographies say Patrick studied for the priesthood under St Germain in Auxerre in France. They also say Patrick, under St Germain's guidance, was involved for a number of years, in missionary work among a group of ancient Celtic people called the Morini who lived in the northwestern part of the region between the Seine and the Rhine rivers.

There was a missionary to the Morini called St Victoricus who was martyred by beheading at Amiens at the end of the fourth century. Perhaps this was the Victoricus that Patrick saw in his Dream.

It's highly likely Patrick would associate the name Victoricus with martyrdom amongst a pagan people.

ST PATRICK'S SIXTH DREAM 'JESUS SPEAKS WITHIN YOU'

The Dream Setting/Backstory

GOD SENT this dream at an unspecified time after *'The Call of The Irish' Dream*.

The Dream Scripture

> Another night – I do not know, God knows, whether it was within me or beside me – I heard authoritative words which I could hear but not understand, until at the end of the speech it became clear: "The one who gave his life for you, he it is who speaks in you"; and I awoke full of joy.

The Problem

There is no specific problem mentioned though Patrick lived in the midst of daily life threatening difficulties. Perhaps God just wanted to bless Patrick with an awareness of the indwelling Jesus and an experience of tongues and interpretation.

The Dreamer's Metron

Saint Patrick was a fifth-century Romano-British Christian missionary and bishop credited with bringing Christianity to parts of Ireland. He baptised thousands of people and ordained many priests to lead the new Christian communities. He converted wealthy women, some of whom became nuns in the face of family opposition.

He also dealt with the sons of kings, converting them too. He also preached to his slavers. Patrick was baptised in the Holy Spirit and fire and spoke in tongues and prophesied. He was also a big dreamer of dreams. Approximately one quarter of Patrick's book, *The Confession* concerns dreams from God that he received and obeyed.

Patrick was also partly responsible for the Christianisation of the Picts and Anglo-Saxons. Although never formally canonised, Patrick became known as the Apostle of Ireland and is venerated as a saint in the

Catholic Church, the Lutheran Church, the Church of Ireland and in the Eastern Orthodox Church where he is regarded as equal-to-the-apostles and Enlightener of Ireland.

Patrick was also a scribe, the first person to write an autobiographical piece in the early Irish church. He strongly opposed slavery and sex trafficking as seen in his, *Letter To The Soldiers of Coroticus*. He also wrote *The Confession*, to counteract accusations made against him.

It's possible the *Letter To The Soldiers of Coroticus* provoked a clerical and political backlash that resulted in the trial which Patrick mentions in *The Confession*.

During his lifetime Patrick's metron was confined to Ireland but in these last days, for some reason, God has increased Patrick's influence all over the world. Perhaps that's why Satan has come up with green beer, hangovers and dancing leprechauns.

The Message

The Message was that Jesus was speaking within Patrick in an unknown tongue. The scripture given explained the dream experience and was most likely part of the interpretation of the unknown tongue.

God's Purpose

God's purpose was to encourage and strengthen Patrick. He also allowed Patrick to experience two gifts of the Holy Spirit in operation - tongues and interpretation of tongues. God also blessed Patrick with a tangible experience of the indwelling Spirit of Jesus Christ interceding within him.

Satan's Purpose

Satan's purpose was to discourage Patrick in his mission. Satan's purpose would have been to keep Patrick unlearned in the gifts of the Holy Spirit. To prevent Patrick from experiencing tongues and interpretation. Satan hates the Holy Spirit's power gifts for they always destroy his kingdom.

Dreamer's Eyes Enlightened

Patrick understood the source and meaning of the dream experience. He understood Jesus was speaking within him in an authoritative unknown language, an unknown tongue.

Dreamer's Response and Application

Patrick accepted the dream experience as being from God and was filled with joy at the thought of Jesus praying within him in an unknown tongue.

Know God Better

God is seen as a loving, caring Heavenly Father who is more than willing to bless His children with the spiritual experience of His presence and the gifts of His Holy Spirit. He is also willing to authenticate His Sons word's that said,

> Anyone who loves me will obey my teaching. My Father will love them, and we will come to them and make our home with them.[1]

The Dream Process

I don't think this is a dream from God. I believe it's a dream from Patrick's own renewed spirit. A dream in which Patrick's regenerated spirit actually allows him to hear Jesus praying within him.

There's a scripture that says the Holy Spirit prays within the renewed Christian,[2] but I can't think of one that says Jesus prays within us. Yet there are plenty that say Jesus lives within a true believer. I can think of ten though there are plenty more.[3] One is when Paul told the Galatians,

> I am crucified with Christ; and it is no longer I who live, but it is Christ who lives in me.[4]

There are also scriptures that speak of Jesus' present day ministry of intercession. One is from Hebrews,

> Now there have been many of those priests, since death prevented them from continuing in office; but because Jesus lives forever, he has a permanent priesthood. Therefore he is able to save completely those who come to God through him, because he always lives to intercede for them.[5]

So if Jesus lives within a renewed Christian and if Jesus ever lives to intercede then it's entirely appropriate for Patrick to hear Jesus within him interceding in a heavenly language, praying in tongues in a language unknown to Patrick.

As noted, Jesus said, On that day you will realise that I am in my Father, and you are in me, and I am in you.[6] This dream is a symbolic visual representation of how this 'You in Me' scripture functions in practice.

This is also a dream with the interpretation of tongues in operation. Initially Patrick didn't know where the authoritative words were coming from or who was speaking them. Then he was told they were coming from the indwelling Jesus who was interceding.

Patrick also couldn't understand the meaning of the words until Jesus gave him part of the interpretation which was, "The one who gave his life for you, he it is who speaks in you".[7] Patrick then woke full of joy.

This dream edifies Patrick with joy. Joy is always a manifestation of the kingdom of God. Paul said, For the kingdom of God is not a matter of eating and drinking, but of righteousness, peace and joy in the Holy Spirit.[8]

Tongues with interpretation always edifies an individual or the church.[9] Paul also said,

> For one who speaks in a tongue does not speak to men but to God; for no one understands, but in his spirit he speaks mysteries.[10]

In this dream Jesus was speaking authoritative words of mystery and prayer to God and not to man. Patrick couldn't understand Him until Jesus gave part the interpretation.

The Usual Suspects

The dream is from God. Jesus is speaking in the Holy Spirit and Satan is defeated.

Takeaways

Jesus is an active intercessor in this dream. Hebrews reminds us of Jesus' role as a priest. It calls Jesus a priest forever in the order of Melchizedek. It also says,

> Because Jesus lives forever, he has a permanent priesthood. Therefore he is able to save completely those who come to God through him, because he always lives to intercede for them. Such a high priest truly meets our need—one who is holy, blameless, pure, set apart from sinners, exalted above the heavens. Unlike the other high priests, he does not need to offer sacrifices day after day, first for his own sins, and then for the sins of the people. He sacrificed for their sins once for all when he offered himself.[11]

This dream begins as a confusing experience for Patrick. Initially he doesn't know the source of the voice nor where the voice is coming from, but at end of the speech everything becomes clear.

The beautiful interpretation is, The one who gave his life for you, he it is who speaks in you.

Patrick was delighted at the reality of this revelation and the experience. He awoke full of joy.

The book of Romans says,

> The kingdom of God is not a matter of eating and drinking, but of righteousness, peace and joy in the Holy Spirit. [12]

Neither Satan or the world can supply real righteousness, peace or joy. Joy is always a manifestation of the Holy Spirit.

Probably the only time a Christian can be 100% sure they are praying in the will of God is when they are speaking in tongues. Often we don't know what way to pray or what to pray about but thankfully the Holy Spirit always makes intersession for the saints according to the will of God. Romans says,

> In the same way, the Spirit helps us in our weakness. We do not know what we ought to pray for, but the Spirit himself intercedes for us through wordless groans. And he who searches our hearts knows the mind of the Spirit, because the Spirit intercedes for God's people in accordance with the will of God.[13]

The wonderful thing about praying in God's will in tongues is knowing our prayers will be answered. John writes,

> This is the confidence we have in approaching God: that if we ask anything according to his will, he hears us. And if we know that he hears us—whatever we ask—we know that we have what we asked of him.[14]

What an encouragement it must have been for Patrick to realise Jesus was praying in an unknown tongue within his own body and spirit. No wonder he was full of joy!

ST PATRICK'S SEVENTH DREAM 'THE SPIRIT HELPS OUR WEAKNESS'

The Dream Setting/Backstory

PATRICK SAID this dream happened at another time. Although he gives no context it seems he was under pressure from Satan who was probably up to his old tricks of accusing and condemning the saints.[1] It's a 'You in Me' dream similar to the previous one. Again the Godhead is praying within Patrick in a language he can't understand. This time the idiom is one of sighs and groans.

The Dream Scripture

> Another time, I saw in me one who was praying. It was as if I were inside my body, and I heard above me, that is, above my inner self. He prayed

strongly, with sighs. I was amazed and astonished, and pondered who it was who prayed in me; but at the end of the prayer, it was clear that it was the Spirit. At this I awoke, and I remembered the apostle saying: "The Spirit helps the weaknesses of our prayer; for we do not know what it is we should pray, but the very Spirit pleads for us with unspeakable sighs, which cannot be expressed in words." And again: The Lord is our advocate, and pleads for us.[2]

The Problem

It seems Satan was condemning and accusing Patrick who didn't know how to respond. So Jesus and the Holy Spirit came to his aid.

The Dreamer's Metron

Saint Patrick was a fifth-century Romano-British Christian missionary and bishop credited with bringing Christianity to parts of Ireland. He baptised thousands of people and ordained many priests to lead the new Christian communities. He converted wealthy women, some of whom became nuns in the face of family opposition.

He also dealt with the sons of kings, converting them too. He also preached to his slavers. Patrick was baptised in the Holy Spirit and fire and spoke in tongues and prophesied. He was also a big dreamer of dreams. Approximately one quarter of Patrick's book, *The Confession* concerns dreams from God that he received and obeyed.

Patrick was also partly responsible for the Christianisation of the Picts and Anglo-Saxons. Although never formally canonised, Patrick became known as the Apostle of Ireland and is venerated as a saint in the Catholic Church, the Lutheran Church, the Church of Ireland and in the Eastern Orthodox Church where he is regarded as equal-to-the-apostles and Enlightener of Ireland.

Patrick was also a scribe, the first person to write an autobiographical piece in the early Irish church. He strongly opposed slavery and sex trafficking as seen in his, *Letter To The Soldiers of Coroticus*. He also wrote *The Confession*, to counteract accusations made against him.

It's possible the *Letter To The Soldiers of Coroticus* provoked a clerical and political backlash that resulted in the trial which Patrick mentions in *The Confession*.

During his lifetime Patrick's metron was confined to Ireland but in these last days, for some reason, God has increased Patrick's influence all over the world. Perhaps that's why Satan has come up with green beer, hangovers and dancing leprechauns.

The Message

The message was, the Holy Spirit was interceding for Patrick and helping him in his weaknesses.

God's Purpose

God's purpose was to protect, support and encourage His servant Patrick in his life and ministry.

Satan's Purpose

Satan's purpose was to wear Patrick down to a point where he couldn't function or minister effectively.

Dreamer's Eyes Enlightened

As in the previous, *Jesus Speaks Within You' Dream*, Patrick initially had no idea what was happening. He was disorientated by this unusual experience of being inside his own body and hearing a voice above him praying strongly, with sighs.

In the end Patrick realised it was God's Holy Spirit who was speaking within him in unspeakable sighs, which cannot be expressed in words. Patrick was then given the interpretation of what was actually happening, when the Holy Spirit brought two scriptures to his remembrance.[3]

Dreamer's Response and Application

Patrick awakens after he realises it was the Holy Spirit who was interceding inside him. Patrick's positive response was to receive two scriptures that explained the dream experience.

Know God Better

God strengthened Patrick and honoured His Son by affirming Jesus' words about the Holy Spirit's work in this present age. The Amplified Bible says,

> However, I am telling you nothing but the truth when I say it is profitable (good, expedient, advantageous) for you that I go away. Because if I do not go away, the Comforter (Counsellor, Helper, Advocate, Intercessor, Strengthener, Standby) will not come to you [into close fellowship with you]; but if I go away, I will send Him

to you [to be in close fellowship with you].[4]

The Dream Process

I don't think this is a dream from God. I believe it's a dream from Patrick's own renewed spirit. A dream in which Patrick's regenerated spirit actually allows him to view the Holy Spirit praying within him as promised in the Bible.[5]

No one can see God[6] but it's possible to see Jesus and the Holy Spirit. For example, the Holy Spirit appeared as a dove at Jesus' baptism and as tongues of fire at Pentecost. In the previous dream Patrick heard but didn't see Jesus.

Jesus promised the Holy Spirit to His disciples. He said, On that day you will realise that I am in my Father, and you are in me, and I am in you.[7] This dream is a symbolic visual representation of how this 'You in Me' scripture functions in practice.

It's also a dream with the interpretation of tongues in operation. It's a complex symbolic dream interpreted by two scriptures the Holy Spirit gave to Patrick, a man deeply entrenched in the Bible.

In this and the previous dream we see Patrick experiencing the Godhead. Here we see the Trinity functioning within Patrick in such a manner that it's hard to tell where One beings and One ends. And of course that's part of the mystery of God.

At the beginning of the dream Patrick said, I saw in me one who was praying. This turns out to be the Holy Spirit.

There were two scriptures given by the indwelling Holy Spirit so Patrick could interpret and understand the dream experience. The first one is,

> And the Holy Spirit helps us in our weakness. For example, we don't know what God wants us to pray for. But the Holy Spirit prays for us with groanings that cannot be expressed in words.[8]

Groanings or sighs that cannot be expressed in words and cannot be understood sounds a lot like speaking in tongues. Paul said,

> For one who speaks in a tongue does not speak to men but to God; for no one understands, but in his spirit he speaks mysteries.[9]

No man or woman can interpret the groanings or the unspeakable sighs of the Holy Spirit but God can. The Bible says,

> The Israelites groaned in their slavery and cried out, and their cry for help because of their slavery went up to God. God

heard their groaning and he remembered his covenant with Abraham, with Isaac and with Jacob. So God looked on the Israelites and was concerned about them.[10]

God is able to interpret unspeakable sighs and groanings and properly respond. God even understands the groanings and sighs of the whole earth and one day when Jesus returns He will set all creation free.[11]

The second scripture Patrick refers to is, The Lord is our advocate, and pleads for us.[12] There are scriptures that call Jesus our advocate and scriptures that call the Holy Spirit our advocate. John mentions one concerning Jesus. He wrote,

> My dear children, I write this to you so that you will not sin. But if anybody does sin, we have an advocate with the Father—Jesus Christ, the Righteous One.[13]

A scripture already mentioned concerning the Holy Spirit as advocate was spoken by Jesus who said,

> "If you love me, keep my commands. And I will ask the Father, and he will give you another advocate to help you and be with you forever— the Spirit of

truth. The world cannot accept him, because it neither sees him nor knows him. But you know him, for he lives with you and will be in you. I will not leave you as orphans; I will come to you. Before long, the world will not see me anymore, but you will see me. Because I live, you also will live. On that day you will realise that I am in my Father, and you are in me, and I am in you. Whoever has my commands and keeps them is the one who loves me. The one who loves me will be loved by my Father, and I too will love them and show myself to them."*14*

This is a very appropriate scripture for Patrick's dream. It fittingly explains what is happening. Overall, this is a dream of edification and guidance that affirms Patrick is constantly supported by God's covering prayers. It also shows Patrick at the centre of God's sovereign will for his life. Paul said,

> And the Father who knows all hearts
> knows what the Spirit is saying, for the
> Spirit pleads for us believers in
> harmony with God's own will. And we
> know that God causes everything to
> work together for the good of those

who love God and are called according to his purpose for them. For God knew his people in advance, and he chose them to become like his Son, so that his Son would be the first-born among many brothers and sisters. And having chosen them, he called them to come to him. And having called them, he gave them right standing with himself. And having given them right standing, he gave them his glory.[15]

In this dream Patrick's renewed spirit gives him the experience of actually being within his own body and seeing the Holy Spirit praying above him. Jonah was in the belly of the whale and Patrick was in his own belly.

The Usual Suspects

Satan was attacking Patrick in his work of spreading the gospel in Ireland. Patrick didn't know what to pray for, so God the Father, Jesus and the Holy Spirit came to his aid.

Takeaways

I often have dreams that are interpreted by a scripture the Holy Spirit immediately brings to mind. A lot of our dreams are in fact scripture in picture form.

Patrick's dream is a clear visual and audible experience of tongues and interpretation as mentioned in Acts 2. In this case the Holy Spirit is speaking but usually it's the believer who does the speaking and it is the Holy Spirit who gives them the words. Acts 2:4 says,

> All of them were filled with the Holy Spirit and began to speak in other tongues as the Spirit enabled them.

It is always the Holy Spirit who gives the interpretation. In this case He uses two scriptures.

Paul says believers who speak in tongues should pray for the power to interpret. He highlights the reason, For if I pray in a tongue, my spirit prays but my mind is unfruitful.[16]

Basically, Paul is saying when someone speaks in tongues their spirit is praying but their mind doesn't understand the meaning unless it is interpreted.

This is what happens in this dream. Initially Patrick was amazed and astonished and had no idea of either the source or the meaning of the unspeakable sighs coming from inside him, until the Holy Spirit revealed it to him.

Tongues just means languages, and sighs and groaning are a credible language to God. In this dream Patrick is shown the process of speaking in tongues happening within himself, occurring inside his own body.

The scripture quoted by Patrick says, The Spirit pleads for us with unspeakable sighs. Other translations say, with inexpressible groanings. Sighs and groanings are the same thing and God understand their meaning.

As I mentioned earlier, we see this in Acts 7:34 which describes a conversation between God and Moses. God says,

> I have indeed seen the oppression of my people in Egypt. I have heard their groaning and have come down to set them free. Now come, I will send you back to Egypt.

Paul when speaking about tongues and interpretation in I Corinthians says,

> There are, it may be, so many kinds of voices in the world, and none of them is without signification.[17]

Sighs and groanings are a credible language to God and Patrick was encouraged and edified when the Holy Spirit gave him the interpretation in the form of two scriptures.

Essentially Patrick is interpreting tongues in this dream. The whole dream is in fact an unusual visual illustration experience of tongues and the interpretation of tongues.

The essential role of the Holy Spirit in Patrick's dream is to encourage Patrick by interceding for him with sighs too deep for words.

Only God can understand the meaning of these unspeakable sighs because God who searches the heart, knows what is the mind of the Spirit, because the Spirit intercedes for the saints according to the will of God.[18]

The Holy Spirit knows the deepest desires and longings of our spirit and makes intercession to God appropriately.

Often our words and our natural understanding are completely inadequate to correctly express the desires, and longings residing in the depths of our being.

Thankfully the Holy Spirit can articulate and convey these yearnings to God in a manner He totally understands.

ST PATRICK'S EIGHTH DREAM 'GOD'S DISPLEASURE'

The Dream Setting/Backstory

WHEN PATRICK BECAME a bishop he was opposed and censured by some of his British superiors who attacked him because of a previously confessed sin he'd committed as a fifteen year old unbeliever.

The Dream Scripture

So on the day I was accused by those I mentioned above, that same night I saw in a vision of the night some writing before my dishonoured face. In the middle of this, I heard an answer from God saying to me: "We have seen with displeasure the face of the one who was chosen deprived of his good name." He did not say: "You have seen with displeasure", but "We have seen with displeasure", as if he were identifying himself with me; as he said "He who touches you as it were touches the pupil of my eye.[1]

The Problem

Patrick's jealous superiors were causing him distress and endangering his Irish mission by calling his fitness for ministry into question because of a teenage misdemeanour Patrick had privately disclosed to a friend.

The Dreamer's Metron

Saint Patrick was a fifth-century Romano-British Christian missionary and bishop credited with bringing Christianity to parts of Ireland. He baptised thousands of people and ordained many priests to lead the new Christian communities. He converted wealthy women, some of whom became nuns in the face of family opposition.

He also dealt with the sons of kings, converting them too. He also preached to his slavers. Patrick was baptised in the Holy Spirit and fire and spoke in tongues and prophesied. He was also a big dreamer of dreams.

Approximately one quarter of Patrick's book, *The Confession* concerns dreams from God that he received and obeyed.

Patrick was also partly responsible for the Christianisation of the Picts and Anglo-Saxons. Although never formally canonised, Patrick became known as the Apostle of Ireland and is venerated as a saint in the Catholic Church, the Lutheran Church, the Church of Ireland and in the Eastern Orthodox Church where he is regarded as equal-to-the-apostles and Enlightener of Ireland.

Patrick was also a scribe, the first person to write an autobiographical piece in the early Irish church. He strongly opposed slavery and sex trafficking as seen in his, *Letter To The Soldiers of Coroticus.* He also wrote *The Confession*, to counteract accusations made against him.

It's possible the *Letter To The Soldiers of Coroticus* provoked a clerical and political backlash that resulted in the trial which Patrick mentions in *The Confession.*

During his lifetime Patrick's metron was confined to Ireland but in these last days, for some reason, God has increased Patrick's influence all over the world. Perhaps that's why Satan has come up with green beer, hangovers and dancing leprechauns.

The Message

Patrick is told God, Jesus and the Holy Spirit are displeased with the behaviour of his superiors who've made him downcast because of their cruel attempt to steal his good name and reputation. God also said He would care for Patrick as the apple of His eye.

God's Purpose

God's purpose was to answer Patrick's distressed prayers and encourage him in his time of need. God wanted Patrick to remember he'd been specifically chosen for God's work in Ireland. God also wanted Patrick to know He was standing with Patrick against the cruel tactics of his superiors.

Satan's Purpose

Satan's purpose was to destroy Patrick's fruitful missionary work in Ireland. He tried this by stirring up disunity and accusation from within the Christian community.

Dreamer's Eyes Enlightened

Patrick clearly understood God was displeased with the accusations against him. He also knew God highly valued him and empathised with him in his predicament.

Dreamer's Response and Application

Patrick was encouraged, edified, and upbuilt by God's affirmation of Patrick's fitness concerning his character and ministry.

Know God Better

God revealed Himself as a loving Father intimately involved with every aspect of Patrick's life. God read the written accusation against Patrick, heard Patrick's prayers and was unhappy that jealousy and legalism had brought dishonour to Patrick. God also affirmed and put into operation His word from Romans,

> There is therefore now no condemnation
> to those who are in Christ Jesus, who
> do not walk according to the flesh, but
> according to the Spirit.[2]

The Dream Process.

This is a symbolic dream of edification and protection in which God makes a statement that Patrick interpreted. There was also some writing before Patrick's face but we're not told anything more about this writing. It was probably the written accusations against Patrick.

As is usual with Patrick the overall dream is also

interpreted through a scripture. In this case Patrick interpreted God's statement to mean that the Trinity viewed Patrick as being like the pupil of God's eye. The words *'as if he were identifying himself with me* causes' Patrick to do this.

This biblical phrase, 'pupil of my eye' or 'apple of my eye' symbolises a person who is highly valued. To be the apple of someone's eye shows you are being intimately focused on and protected. There are four mentions of this phrase in the Old Testament.[3] A couple are, King David asked God to,

> Keep me as the apple of the eye;
> Hide me in the shadow of Your wings.[4]

And Zechariah said,

> For this is what the Lord of Hosts says:
> "After His Glory has sent Me against
> the nations that have plundered you—
> for whoever touches you touches the
> apple of His eye.[5]

The Usual Suspects

Satan is seen in the accusations of Patrick's superiors. God, Jesus and the Holy Spirit are evident in the phrase, We have seen with displeasure . . .

Takeaways

The truth is, we are all sinners and Satan accuses, Jesus defends, and the Holy Spirit convicts us of our sin. Accusation always condemns and paralyses while Godly conviction enables us to move forward into God's plans and purpose.

Patrick, who was in constant prayer on behalf of the Irish, knew prayer was not just the simple asking of God for things. He knew by experience that prayer is always about spiritual conflict. When we pray, we intimately engage with the Lord, but we are also contesting powers of darkness who do their damnedest to resist us.

When we pray we are often shifting these powers of heaven so that God's Kingdom will can be accomplished on earth. So, we shouldn't be surprised when we encounter pushback, but it's never pleasant.

When Nehemiah was rebuilding the walls of Jerusalem he encouraged the workers. He said,

> Then as I looked over the situation, I called together the nobles and the rest of the people and said to them, "Don't be afraid of the enemy! Remember the Lord, who is great and glorious, and fight for your brothers, your sons, your daughters, your wives, and your homes.[6]

Instead of encouraging and fighting for their brothers like Nehemiah, the jealous British bishops did the work of Satan and condemned Patrick. The is the worst betrayal of all.

Yet, as with Jacob in his Covenant Dream, concerning the stairway to heaven God also assured Patrick of His continual support and love in the midst of fraternal rivalry.

God did the choosing and He made sure His servant Patrick would be protected and would finish the race.

ANOTHER DREAM?

WE KNOW nothing credible about Patrick apart from his writings, but his writings are enough. We don't know with certainty where Patrick came from nor do we know the actual location of any place where he actually lived or ministered in Ireland.

But we do know Patrick lived his life and ministry based on the word of God and being led by the Holy Spirit.

We also know Patrick was a man of constant prayer, filled with the Holy Spirit, who functioned in various charismatic gifts, especially prophecy, miracles, tongues and interpretation of tongues, healings, dreams and visions and interpretation of dreams and visions.

We also know Patrick spent his last thirty years in Ireland, preaching the gospel of Jesus Christ, baptising pagans, ordaining priests, and founding churches and monasteries.

His legacy is remarkable because Ireland was fully converted to Christianity within two centuries, and was the only nation in all of Europe to do so peacefully.

Thomas Cahill called his bestselling book, *How the Irish Saved Civilisation*. Cahill may well have named it, *How St Patrick Saved Civilisation,* because Patrick's anointing and sphere of influence extended well beyond Ireland.

Cahill claims Patrick and his heritage enabled Western learning to survive the destruction of the Dark Ages, because while the rest of Europe floundered in fear and superstition Patrick's monasteries copied and preserved the classical texts.

Then years later, Irish monks returned this knowledge back into Europe by establishing monasteries and communities in England, Germany, France, Switzerland, and Italy.

When Patrick first arrived in Ireland three hundred gods and goddesses held the nation in captivity. A few centuries later the old gods were banished and druidism, human sacrifice and slavery were finished. Ireland then became known as, *The Land of Saints and Scholars.*

Jesus told a parable about deliverance. He said,

> When an impure spirit comes out of a
> person, it goes through arid places
> seeking rest and does not find it. Then
> it says, 'I will return to the house I left.'

When it arrives, it finds the house unoccupied, swept clean and put in order. Then it goes and takes with it seven other spirits more wicked than itself, and they go in and live there. And the final condition of that person is worse than the first. That is how it will be with this wicked generation.[1]

The story is usually viewed as a cautionary tale about a possessed individual who was once delivered but subsequently became repossessed again. That, of course, is an appropriate interpretation but it's not what Jesus was talking about here. Read the last line of the parable again.

Jesus was actually talking about an entire generation of people being repossessed once again by demon gods that returned to their former habitations. This generation of people actually ended up in a far worse condition than they were in originally.

In context, this means a post-Christian nation or civilisation could actually end up in more bondage than when they were a pre-Christian country.

Today, Ireland is rapidly becoming a post-Christian nation. The druids are back in fashion, slavery has returned in the form of sex trafficking and human sacrifice is back in the guise of abortion.

Maybe we need another Patrick or Patricks or Patricias, saints filled with the Holy Spirit who know God's word and who know how to hear God's voice in dreams and visions.

Perhaps we need Ireland's dreamers to rise up again and *The Voice of the Irish* to be heard once more in our land for we are the music makers and we are the dreamers of dreams.

THE DREAMS SCRIPTURES

These dream scriptures are taken from St Patrick's Confession. The C stands for the chapter. So C16 means Chapter 16.

C16 - After I arrived in Ireland, I tended sheep every day, and I prayed frequently during the day. More and more the love of God increased, and my sense of awe before God. Faith grew, and my spirit was moved, so that in one day I would pray up to one hundred times, and at night perhaps the same. I even remained in the woods and on the mountain, and I would rise to pray before dawn in snow and ice and rain. I never felt the worse for it, and I never felt lazy – as I realise now, the spirit was burning in me at that time.

. . .

C17. You Have Fasted Well Dream

It was there one night in my sleep that I heard a voice saying to me: "You have fasted well. Very soon you will return to your native country."

C17. Your Ship Is Ready Dream - Again after a short while, I heard a someone saying to me: "Look – your ship is ready." It was not nearby, but a good two hundred miles away. I had never been to the place, nor did I know anyone there. So I ran away then, and left the man with whom I had been for six years. It was in the strength of God that I went – God who turned the direction of my life to good; I feared nothing while I was on the journey to that ship.

C18 - The day I arrived, the ship was about to leave the place. I said I needed to set sail with them, but the captain was not at all pleased. He replied unpleasantly and angrily: "Don't you dare try to come with us." When I heard that, I left them and went back to the hut where I had lodgings. I began to pray while I was going; and before I even finished the prayer, I heard one of them shout aloud at me: "Come quickly – those men are calling you!" I turned back right away, and they began to say to me: "Come – we'll trust you. Prove you're our friend in any way you wish." That day, I refused to suck their breasts, because of my reverence for God. They were pagans, and I hoped they might come to faith in Jesus Christ. This is how I got to go with them, and we set sail right away.

C19 - After three days we made it to land, and then for twenty eight days we travelled through a wilderness. Food ran out, and great hunger came over them. The captain turned to me and said: "What about this, Christian? You tell us that your God is great and all-powerful – why can't you pray for us, since we're in a bad state with hunger? There's no sign of us finding a human being anywhere!" Then I said to them with some confidence: "Turn in faith with all your hearts to the Lord my God, because nothing is impossible for him, so that he may put food in your way – even enough to make you fully satisfied! He has an abundance everywhere." With the help of God, this is actually what happened! A herd of pigs appeared in the way before our eyes! They killed many of them and there they remained for two nights, and were fully restored, and the dogs too were filled. Many of them had grown weak and left half-alive by the way. After this, they gave the greatest of thanks to God, and I was honoured in their eyes. From this day on, they had plenty of food. They also found some wild honey, and offered some of it to me. However, one of them said: "This honey must have been offered in sacrifice to a god." Thanks be to God, from then on I tasted none of it.

C20 - Satan Tested Patrick Dream - That same night while I was sleeping, Satan strongly put me to the test – I will remember it as long as I live! It was as if an enormous rock fell on me, and I lost all power in my limbs. Although I knew little about the life of the spirit at the time, how was it that I knew to call upon Helias? While these things were happening, I saw the sun rise in the sky, and while I was calling "Helias! Helias!" with all my strength, the splendour of the sun fell on me; and immediately, all that weight was lifted from me. I believe that I was helped by Christ the Lord, and that his spirit cried out for me. I trust that it will be like this whenever I am under stress, as the gospel says: "In that day, the Lord testifies, it will not be you who will speak, but the Spirit of your Father who speaks in you."

C21 - Two Months In Captivity Dream - It happened again after many years that I was taken a prisoner. On the first night I was with them, I heard a divine answer saying to me: "You will be with them for two months." This is how it was: on the sixtieth night, the Lord freed me from their hands.

C22 - While we were still on the journey, the Lord provided food and fire and shelter every day until we met some people on the tenth day. As I mentioned above, we travelled for twenty eight days through the wilderness. On the very night we met people, we ran out of food.

C23 - The Call of The Irish Dream - A few years later I was again with my parents in Britain. They welcomed me as a son, and they pleaded with me that, after all the many tribulations I had undergone, I should never leave them again. It was while I was there that I saw, in a vision in the night, a man whose name was Victoricus coming as it were from Ireland with so many letters they could not be counted. He gave me one of these, and I read the beginning of the letter, the voice of the Irish people. While I was reading out the beginning of the letter, I thought I heard at that moment the voice of those who were beside the wood of Voclut, near the western sea. They called out as it were with one voice: "We beg you, holy boy, to come and walk again among us." This touched my heart deeply, and I could not read any further; I woke up then. Thanks be to God, after many years the Lord granted them what they were calling for.

C24 - Jesus Speaks Within You Dream - Another night – I do not know, God knows, whether it was within me or beside me – I heard authoritative words which I could hear but not understand, until at the end of the speech it became clear: "The one who gave his life for you, he it is who speaks in you"; and I awoke full of joy.

C25 - The Spirit Helps Our Weakness Dream - Another time, I saw in me one who was praying. It was as if I were inside my body, and I heard above me, that is, above my inner self. He prayed strongly, with sighs. I was amazed and astonished, and pondered who it was who prayed in me; but at the end of the prayer, it was clear that it was the Spirit. At this I awoke, and I remembered the apostle saying: "The Spirit helps the weaknesses of our prayer; for we do not know what it is we should pray, but the very Spirit pleads for us with unspeakable sighs, which cannot be expressed in words." And again: "The Lord is our advocate, and pleads for us."

C26 - One time I was put to the test by some superiors of mine. They came and put my sins against my hard work as a bishop. This hit me very hard, so much so that it seemed I was about to fall, both here and in eternity. But the Lord in his kindness spared the converts and the strangers for the sake of his name, and strongly supported me when I was so badly treated. I did not slip into sin and disgrace. I pray that God not hold this sin against them.

. . .

C27 -They brought up against me after thirty years something I had already confessed before I was a deacon. What happened was that, one day when I was feeling anxious and low, with a very dear friend of mine I referred to some things I had done one day – rather, in one hour – when I was young, before I overcame my weakness. I don't know – God knows – whether I was then fifteen years old at the time, and I did not then believe in the living God, not even when I was a child. In fact, I remained in death and unbelief until I was reproved strongly, and actually brought low by hunger and nakedness daily.

C28 - My defence was that I remained on in Ireland, and that not of my own choosing, until I almost perished. However, it was very good for me, since God straightened me out, and he prepared me for what I would be today. I was far different then from what I am now, and I have care for others, and I have enough to do to save them. In those days I did not even have concern for my own welfare.

C29 - God's Displeasure Dream - So on the day I was accused by those I mentioned above, that same night I saw in a vision of the night some writing before my dishonoured face. In the middle of this, I heard an answer from God saying to me: "We have seen with displeasure the face of the one who was chosen deprived of his good name." He did not say: "You have seen with displeasure", but "We have seen with displeasure", as if he were identifying himself with me; as he said "He who touches you as it were touches the pupil of my eye."

C30 - For that reason, I give thanks to the one who strengthened me in all things, so that he would not impede me in the course I had undertaken and from the works also which I had learned from Christ my Lord. Rather, I sensed in myself no little strength from him, and my faith passed the test before God and people.

C31 - I make bold to say that my conscience does not blame me, now and in the future. I have God for witness that I have not told lies in the account I have given you.

C32 - But I grieve more for my very dear friend, that we had to hear such an account – the one to whom I entrusted my very soul. I did learn from some brothers before the case was heard that he came to my defence in my absence. I was not there at the time, not even in Britain, and it was not I who brought up the matter. In fact it was he himself who told me from his own mouth:

"Look, you are being given the rank of bishop." That is something I did not deserve. How could he then afterwards come to disgrace me in public before all, both good and bad, about a matter for which he had already freely and joyfully forgiven me, as indeed had God, who is greater than all?

NOTES

2. SAINTS & SCHOLARS

1. James 1:17
2. Romans 11:29
3. 2 Timothy 1:6
4. Romans 6:22
5. Isaiah 11:2
6. Psalm 127:3
7. Proverbs 18:22
8. Genesis 1:29
9. Proverbs 12:26
10. James 1:17
11. Ephesians 4:11-13
12. 1 Corinthians 12:4-11
13. 1 Corinthians 12:28
14. Romans 12:4-8
15. 1 Peter 4:10-11
16. 1 Kings 19:18

3. THE WORLD'S FAVOURITE SAINT

1. The Letter to the Soldiers of Coroticus

4. TWO SAINT PATRICKS

1. https://en.wikipedia.org/wiki/Hagiography
2. 2 Peter 1:16 (AMP)

5. THE HOLY SPIRIT

1. John 2:27
2. C45
3. C4
4. C41
5. C33

6. PATRICK'S SIMPLE STORY

1. C16

7. ST PATRICK'S EIGHT DREAMS

1. Jeremiah 1:10
2. C17
3. C17
4. C20
5. C21
6. C24
7. C24
8. C25
9. C29

8. HOW JESUS INTERPRETS DREAMS

1. Mark 4:1-20
2. Daniel 1:17
3. Daniel 2:31-35
4. Daniel 2:38-45
5. Genesis 40:8
6. Daniel 2:27-28
7. Daniel 2:29-30
8. Judges 7:13-14

9. NOTES ON PATRICK'S DREAMS

1. Romans 8:29
2. C17
3. C17
4. C20
5. C21
6. C23
7. C24
8. C25
9. C29
10. C23 – 29. Daniel 7:2, 7:13.
11. C17, C21, C 29.
12. Romans 8:26
13. C29
14. 1 Ephesians 1:11
15. Isaiah 53:11
16. John 14:17
17. John 14:23
18. 1 Corinthians 6:19–20
19. Matthew 20:10
20. Matthew 20:10 (NLT)
21. Romans 8:26-28
22. John 14:25
23. John 14:25-27

10. PRAYING IN TONGUES DREAMS

1. 1 Corinthians 14:27
2. 1 Corinthians 14:23
3. 1 Corinthians 14:3-4
4. 1 John 5:14-15
5. Romans 8:27
6. Ezekiel 22:30
7. Matthew 9:37-38
8. John 14:15-21
9. John 14:20

11. SIX SOURCES OF DREAMS

1. Jeremiah 23:26
2. Jeremiah 29:8
3. Jeremiah 23:32
4. Deuteronomy 13:1-3
5. Jeremiah 23:29
6. Jeremiah 23:25-32
7. Jude 1:8
8. Isaiah 29:7-8
9. Ecclesiastes 5:3
10. John 14:23-24
11. 1 Corinthians 6:17
12. 1 Corinthians 14:3
13. John 14:26
14. 1 Corinthians 3:1-3
15. Isaiah 49:16
16. 1 Thessalonians 5:11
17. Ephesians 1:17-19
18. Proverbs 20:27
19. 1 Corinthians 2:11
20. 1 Corinthians 7:10-12
21. 1 Corinthians 7:39-40
22. John 14:23-24
23. 1 Corinthians 2:14
24. James 3:13-18
25. James 3:17
26. James.3:15
27. Ecclesiastes 5:3
28. Ephesians 4:17-19
29. Colossians 3:2

13. UNDER THE MICROSCOPE

1. Ephesians 1:15-23

14. ST PATRICK'S METRON

1. 2 Corinthians 10:12-18

15. THE MCCAULEY DREAM CHECKLIST

1. Ephesians 1:17-19
2. Psalm 46:1-2
3. Ephesians 3:6
4. Daniel 8:26
5. Hebrews 1:3
6. Ephesians 3:6
7. Ephesians 3:10
8. John 10:10
9. Luke 22:31
10. 1 Peter 5:8
11. Ephesians 1:17
12. Revelation 11:15
13. Luke 24:13-35

16. ST PATRICK'S FIRST DREAM 'YOU HAVE FASTED WELL'

1. C16
2. Isaiah 58:6-7
3. Isaiah 61:1-3

17. ST PATRICK'S SECOND DREAM 'YOUR SHIP IS READY'

1. Genesis 22:18
2. Genesis 3:15
3. Matthew 4:4
4. Romans 10:17
5. C17

18. ST PATRICK'S THIRD DREAM 'SATAN TESTED PATRICK'

1. Deuteronomy 31:6, Hebrews 13:5
2. John 10:10
3. 1 John 3:8
4. Acts 10:38
5. C19
6. Zechariah 4:6
7. Matthew 10:18-20
8. Matthew 10:20 (ESV)
9. John 14:26
10. Matthew 26:12
11. Matthew 27:46
12. Matthew 10:20
13. 1 Corinthians 13:1
14. Matthew 10:20
15. Malachi 4:1-6
16. Malachi 4:2 (NLT)
17. C60

20. ST PATRICK'S FIFTH DREAM 'THE CALL OF THE IRISH'

1. C23
2. C23

21. ST PATRICK'S SIXTH DREAM 'JESUS SPEAKS WITHIN YOU'

1. John 14:23
2. Romans 8:26-27
3. John 14:23, Romans 8:10, 2 Corinthians 4:6-7, Galatians 1:15-16, Galatians 2:20, Galatians 4:19, Ephesians 4:17, Colossians 1:27, 2 Thessalonians 1:10.
4. Galatians 2:20

5. Hebrews 7:25
6. John 14:20
7. C24
8. Romans 14:17
9. 1 Corinthians 14:5
10. 1 Corinthians 14:2 (NASB)
11. Hebrews 7:24-27
12. Romans 14:17-18
13. Romans 8:26-27
14. John 5:14-15

22. ST PATRICK'S SEVENTH DREAM 'THE SPIRIT HELPS OUR WEAKNESS'

1. Revelation 12:10
2. C25
3. John 14:26
4. John 16:7 (AMPC)
5. Romans 8:26
6. John 1:18
7. John 14:20
8. Romans 8:26 (NLT)
9. 1 Corinthians 14:2 (NASB)
10. Exodus 2:24-25
11. Romans 8:22-23
12. C25
13. 1 John 2:1
14. John 14:15-17
15. Romans 8:27-29
16. 1 Corinthians 14:14
17. 1 Corinthians 14:10
18. 8:26–27

23. ST PATRICK'S EIGHTH DREAM
'GOD'S DISPLEASURE'

1. C29
2. Romans 8:1
3. Psalm 17:8, Zechariah 2:8, Deuteronomy 32:10, Proverbs 7:2
4. Psalm 17:8
5. Zechariah 2:8
6. Nehemiah 4:14-20

24. ANOTHER DREAM?

1. Matthew 12:43-45

Printed in Great Britain
by Amazon